The Power of FLOUR

Bob's Red Mill®

To Your Good Health®

Bob Moore

Cooking with Non-traditional Flours

by Tiffany Haugen

The Power of FLOUR

Bob's Red Mill®

To Your Good Health®

Bob Moore

Cooking with Non-traditional Flours

by Tiffany Haugen

Frank Amato

PORTLAND

Dedication

This book is dedicated to my family and friends. It is their willingness to always try something new that inspired every recipe in this book.

About the Author

After writing multiple cookbooks focusing on plank cooking, grilling, and smoking foods, Tiffany Haugen has finally turned her passion for baking and nutritional research into this exciting cookbook.

A Master's degree in health education, culinary travels that have spanned the globe, seminar presentations, and being a food columnist for several outdoor publications have built a solid background for this fresh, imaginative author.

Tiffany's cooking skills stem from a lifetime of practical experience, and her passion for healthy cooking is contagious. As one would expect, the style in which Tiffany presents her creative recipes is concise and easy to follow; after all, her goal is to save the world, one cookie at a time.

Tiffany lives with her husband Scott, and two sons Braxton and Kazden in the western Oregon town in which she grew up.

All inquiries should be addressed to:
Frank Amato Publications, Inc.
P.O. Box 82112
Portland, Oregon 97282
www.amatobooks.com
(503) 653-8108
1-800-541-9498

BOB'S RED MILL is a registered trademark of Bob's Red Mill Natural Foods
Published under license from Bob's Red Mill Natural Foods, Milwaukie, OR

Photographs: Tiffany Haugen
Cover and book design: Tony Amato

ISBN-13: 978-1-57188-445-9   UPC: 0-81127-00280-1

Printed in Hong Kong

10 9 8 7 6 5 4 3 2 1

Table of Contents

Table of Contents

Breads 34

Healthy Snacks................72

Table of Contents

Desserts 96

Foreword

One well-chosen word is inadequate to explain an experience, and Tiffany Haugen's *The Power of Flour* is an experience. Three words maybe? Innovative. Joyous. Enlightening.

Seldom have I experienced such approachable recipe innovation based on world travel, kids' tastes and a passion for superb nutrition. Joy of life sharing food with family and friends exudes from every recipe. The reader is enlightened by common sense recipes that use numerous flours from unusual grains.

Tiffany Haugen has produced a needed, reliable and valued collection of family kitchen recipes that will both nourish and create endless conversation based on the reader's new-found knowledge and skills.

This book incorporates many of the superb flours we manufacture at Bob's Red Mill®. I own a copy. It is a treasure.

—*Dennis Gilliam*
Executive Vice President, Sales and Marketing
Bob's Red Mill Natural Foods, Inc.

Introduction

My earliest baking memory is making pies in my grandmother's kitchen. She always gave us our own dough to roll and taught us how to make the dough scraps into buttery, cinnamon and sugar crisps.

Next, I recall the marathon brownie and chocolate chip cookie baking sessions with my grade school friends. They loved coming to my house to bake and my gracious mom never minded cleaning up after us.

I think the most fun I ever had baking was while living in a very remote Inupiat Eskimo village in Alaska's arctic, where my husband and I were school teachers. In my enthusiasm to introduce the idea of a "cakewalk," I ended up making nearly 50 individually decorated cakes for the event.

With a degree in health education and promotion, I have always been drawn to the study of nutrition. Having children was the catalyst I needed to bring my two passions together—baking and nutrition.

Although my previous cookbooks to date have been primarily based on grilling, planking, and smoking foods—both wild and domestic fish and game—this is my first baking book. Many of these recipes were developed when I needed a "creative baking break" while working on other books. I've never been so excited about a cookbook, if for no other reason than to raise nutritional awareness in people.

—*Tiffany Haugen*

Why Use Nutritious Flours?

The most important reason for using nutritious flours is the direct health benefits. But nutritious flours also add a deeper flavor and texture than foods made with less healthy ingredients.

Proven health benefits of nutritious flours include reduced risks of bowel disorders, cancers, heart disease and high cholesterol, stroke, high blood pressure, obesity and type 2 diabetes.

Some nutritious flours are also known to prevent gallstones and blood vessel damage. They can improve blood flow, reduce asthma and migraine headaches.

Nutritional flours also provide energy and endurance and can strengthen the immune system. Some studies have shown that symptoms of depression can decrease with the use of nutritious flours. See Appendix A (page 128) for more information on nutritious flours.

With the newer dietary guidelines stressing the importance of eating more whole grains, it is easy to see how quickly the food industry has attempted to make processed foods healthier. Home cooks need to do the same. We need to add more protein, fiber, vitamins and minerals to our home-baked goods to get the most out of every item we are eating. We owe it to ourselves, our families and the people for whom we cook.

Cooking and baking at home doesn't always mean long hours spent laboring over a hot stove or oven. Many of the pleasures of baking come with making items that can be enjoyed for several days or frozen and reheated for a quick snack.

There are also some great kitchen gadgets that make baking easy and no fuss: bread machines, standing mixers, and food processors, are just a few.

The goal of this cookbook is to expand the horizons of not only the cooks preparing the food, but also for the people eating the food to enjoy new culinary experiences.

The food prepared from the recipes in this book will not taste like soft, fluffy, flavorless, enriched white flour products. They are not enhanced with preservatives and flavoring agents. They were developed as a mode to deliver healthy ingredients and introduce new, exciting flavors and tastes.

When embarking on the journey to add healthy flours to commonly cooked and baked items, I started slow. It took a little bit of skill with mathematical fractions, but taking some of my favorite friend- and family-tested recipes, I used the 1-2-3 approach.

The first step in cooking with nutritious flours is to get a few of them

into the pantry. Just replacing a few tablespoons of white flour in favorite recipes gives a nutritional boost.

My experience with this gradual approach turned several people on to the deeper flavors and textures nutritious flours bring to a recipe. In fact, I had some testers passing up morning doughnuts in the hope that the afternoon would bring some kind of a whole-grain, nutrient-packed sweet treat for them to try.

The biggest surprises came with my children and their friends. Many of them enjoyed taking the time to try new things and analyze the flavors. We openly discussed how some flavors such as chocolate, mask stronger flavored flours and give some of the foods an "anything goes" feeling.

The 1-2-3 approach can also be friendlier on the food budget. Instead of buying one of every flour on the list, then wondering what to do with them all, buy three or four of the ones that intrigue you most and start adding them to your own recipes.

Many of the recipes in this book offer substitution suggestions. Calling for spelt or whole wheat flour, barley or oat flour, this book was written to promote experimentation.

1-2-3 Approach

If a recipe calls for 3 cups white flour, make it the first time with a combination of 1 cup whole wheat or spelt flour to 2 cups white flour. Once that has been "approved" (or eaten in one afternoon), make a note to "up the anty" next go around.

When making that recipe again add 1 cup whole wheat or spelt, 1 cup white flour and add an additional nutritious flour.

The third time, make the recipe and omit the white flour altogether, substituting it with a combination of nutritious flours instead. Always make sure to accommodate for lower or gluten-free flours by adding extra starch.

Many times these edited recipes will turn out looking quite different from their white-flour counterparts, but in most cases, they will taste better. And if recipes don't turn out as planned, see my Recipe Rescue in Appendix B (page 129).

Along the same lines of nutritious flour replacement comes replacement of other items such as fats, sweeteners and liquids. See Appendix C (page 130). Depending on diet restrictions and food allergies/sensitivities, almost any recipe in this book can be adapted to fit a particular situation.

Soups,
Salads & Pastas

Make your meal starter a conversation starter. These recipes are enjoyable ways to introduce different types of flours in some rather unconventional ways. The soups and dressings can also be used as chip dips or baked potato toppers. Thin or thicken to desired texture, add your favorite spices and most importantly, have fun with healthy flours!

Peas In A Pod Soup

Based on an old family recipe, this soup can be served thick as a side dish or thinned down as a soup. The combination of the wholesome taste of traditional split-pea soup with the fresh taste of garden peas is delicious.

- 6 slices bacon, chopped
- 2 cups onion, diced
- 1/3 cup green pea flour
- 3 cups chicken or vegetable broth
- 1-2 cups peas, fresh or frozen
- Salt and pepper to taste

In a large soup pot, fry bacon until browned. Add onions and sauté until caramelized, 10-20 minutes. In a separate bowl combine broth with green pea flour, whisk until smooth. Add mixture to soup pot, bring to a low boil. Lower heat and simmer 25-30 minutes. Add fresh or frozen peas during the last 10 minutes of cooking. Thin soup with additional broth or water if needed. Salt and pepper to taste.

Get Nutty Soup

- 1 cup onion, chopped
- 4 cloves garlic, chopped
- 2 tablespoons butter
- 2 tablespoons coconut flour
- 2 tablespoons fava or garbanzo bean flour
- 1/4 cup almond meal/flour
- 3 cups chicken or vegetable broth
- 1 14-ounce can coconut milk
- 1/3 cup peanut butter
- 1 15-ounce can pumpkin puree
- 1 teaspoon curry powder
- 1/2 teaspoon coriander
- 1/2 teaspoon ginger
- Salt and white pepper to taste
- Fresh cilantro for garnish

In a large soup pot, sauté onions in butter until tender. Add garlic, sautéing an additional 1-2 minutes on medium heat. In a separate bowl combine broth with flours, whisk until smooth. Add mixture to soup pot along with all remaining ingredients. Bring to a low boil. Lower heat and simmer 25-30 minutes. Thin soup with additional broth or water if needed. Salt and white pepper to taste. Garnish with cilantro if desired.

When fall brings the first chill in the air, this is the first soup I make. Combining the flavors of peanut butter and coconut milk, this hearty soup is rich and filling. Sweet potato or winter squash puree can be substituted for the pumpkin as they both make healthy alternatives.

Tortilla Soup

There are countless versions of tortilla soup. This one can be thickened and used as a dip and other bean flours can be substituted for flavor variations. Not until I nicknamed it Dorito Soup, would my kids even try it. Now it is a favorite, especially if they can top it with extras like grated cheddar cheese, sour cream, crunched-up corn chips and guacamole.

- 1 cup boiling water
- 1/4 cup corn meal, medium grind
- 2 tablespoons olive oil
- 1 cup bell pepper, diced
- 1 cup onion, diced
- 1 package taco seasoning
- 6 cups turkey or chicken broth
- 1 cup black or pinto bean flour
- 1 10.75-ounce can condensed tomato soup
- 2 cups cooked boneless turkey or chicken, shredded
- 1 1/2 cups corn

In a small bowl soak corn meal in 1 cup boiling water. In a large soup pot, sauté onions and peppers in olive oil until tender. Add seasoning, sautéing an additional 1-2 minutes on medium heat. In a separate bowl combine broth with bean flour, whisk until smooth. Add corn and bean mixtures to soup pot. Bring to a low boil. Lower heat and simmer 25-30 minutes. Add tomato soup, meat and corn, cooking an additional 15 minutes. Salt and pepper to taste.

Longevity Soup

*I*t's the anti-inflammatory flavorings in this soup that give it its name. Your body can't help but feel great after a few bowls of this. For a soup with more texture, add the beans and/or meat after the soup is blended. Cooked grains such as rye, barley or brown rice can also be added.

- 1 quart chicken or vegetable broth
- 6 cups veggies (cauliflower, broccoli, zucchini, peppers, onion, carrots, etc.)
- 1/2 cup black bean flour
- 4 cloves of garlic
- 1-2 cups lean meat or tofu, sliced or cubed (optional)
- 1-2 cans beans (black, garbanzo, white, pinto, etc.)
- 1-2 teaspoons each spice (depending on the flavor you are going for: turmeric, chili powder, paprika, lemon pepper, cumin, and/or crushed red pepper)
- 1-3 tablespoons extra-virgin olive oil (optional)

In a large soup pot combine broth with chopped veggies. Add enough water to cover the veggies. Salt to taste. Cook over medium heat until veggies are tender. Add meat or tofu if desired. Using an immersion blender or regular blender, blend all soup ingredients until smooth. Wisk in black bean flour. Cook 10-15 minutes on medium heat. Add cooked beans. Add spices and adjust taste accordingly. Remove soup from heat and add extra virgin olive oil if desired.

- 3 tablespoons olive oil
- 2 cups onion, chopped
- 4 cloves garlic
- 8 cups dark green, leafy vegetables (spinach, kale, chard, turnip or mustard greens)
- 2 quarts chicken, beef or vegetable broth
- 1/2 cup fava or garbanzo bean flour
- 2 tablespoons green pea flour (optional)
- 1/2 cup fresh herbs (basil, parsley, chives and/or cilantro)

In a large soup pot, sauté onions in olive oil until tender. Add garlic and greens, sautéing an additional 5-7 minutes on medium heat. In a separate bowl combine broth with bean and/or pea flour, whisk until smooth. Add mixture to soup pot. Bring to a low boil then lower heat and simmer 10 minutes. Add fresh herbs and cook an additional 5 minutes. Using an immersion blender or regular blender, blend all soup ingredients until smooth. Salt and pepper to taste.

When living overseas, jet-lag was a regular ailment. Feeling my body needed an extra boost from all the stresses of travel, this soup always delivered. Vary greens and herbs for many different flavor combinations.

Soup Sticks

The idea came from a friend who suggested I adapt my biscotti recipe to a savory, cracker-type snack. These sticks are specifically designed for dunking, and any soup is sure to benefit from them. Any type of nuts can be used and seasonings can also be varied.

- 1/3 cup butter, softened
- 2 eggs, beaten
- 2 tablespoons water
- 1 tablespoon sugar
- 1 cup whole wheat or spelt flour
- 1/2 cup rye flour
- 1 teaspoon baking powder
- 1 teaspoon salt
- 1/2 teaspoon Italian Seasoning
- 1/4 cup pine nuts, chopped
- 1/2 cup sundried tomatoes in oil, chopped
- 1/2 cup parmesan cheese, grated

Preheat oven to 350°. In a large bowl, cream first four ingredients until smooth. In a small bowl combine remaining ingredients, mixing well. Add dry ingredients to wet ingredients, mixing until combined. Shape dough into two long loaves (about 4" by 10") on a baking sheet. Bake 20 minutes. Remove from the oven and slice on the diagonal into 1" slices. Turn slices cut-side down and return to oven, baking an additional 10-15 minutes or until crisp and lightly browned.

South-Of-The-Border Salad

Based on my mother-in-laws favorite meal of hot chili over salad greens, this recipe brings a new twist to salad. The Hot Black Bean Dressing actually wilts the greens, giving them a texture that is much like a traditional spinach salad.

- 6 cups salad greens
- 1-2 cups corn
- 1 red onion, diced
- 2 tomatoes, chopped
- 1/2 jicama, chopped
- 1 bell pepper, chopped
- 1/2 cup fresh cilantro leaves

Hot Black Bean Dressing:
- 1/2 cup black bean flour
- 2 cups chicken or vegetable broth
- 1 teaspoon chili powder
- 1 teaspoon cumin
- 1/4 teaspoon onion powder
- Dash of cayenne
- 1 teaspoon vinegar
- 2 teaspoons olive oil

In a small saucepan, whisk bean flour into broth. Bring to a low boil. Lower heat and simmer 15 minutes, stirring often. While the dressing is cooking, divide salad ingredients on 4-8 plates (depending on serving size). Add additional spices to dressing, continue to simmer 5 minutes. Remove from heat, adding vinegar and olive oil. Thin with water or broth if needed. Salt and pepper to taste. Serve warm over South-Of-The-Border Salad.

Bouncing Ball Salad

- 1/2 cup fava bean flour
- 1/2 cup garbanzo bean flour
- 3 cups water
- 1/2 cup millet flour
- 1/3 cup onion, minced
- 1/3 cup flat-leaf parsley, minced
- 1/3 cup cilantro, minced

- 2 cloves garlic, minced
- 1 teaspoon baking powder
- 1 teaspoon salt
- 1 teaspoon ground cumin
- 1/2 teaspoon turmeric
- 1/4 teaspoon cayenne pepper
- Canola oil for frying

In a medium saucepan, slowly whisk flours into boiling water. Cook 10 minutes stirring constantly to avoid lumps. Set aside to cool. In a mixing bowl, combine remaining ingredients. Add cooled bean mixture, mix well adding water if necessary. Mixture should be able to hold together for frying. In a large skillet, heat 1 inch of oil. Scoop rounded tablespoons of the falafel mixture into hot oil and fry until browned and crisp, about 2 minutes per side. Place on paper towels to drain. Serve warm with Tahini Sauce.

Tahini Sauce:
- 1/2 cup tahini (sesame seed paste)
- 3 gloves garlic, crushed
- 1 teaspoon salt

- 2 tablespoons olive oil
- 1/4 cup lemon juice
- 1 tablespoon parsley

In a food processor or mini-chopper, blend all ingredients until thoroughly combined.

Quite possibly my favorite fast food, I have never met a falafel I didn't like. These falafel, from scratch, are sure to tantalize your taste buds. They don't actually bounce, but my kids loved the name. Serve with homemade or prepared tahini sauce for dipping.

Go Greek Salad

resh and crisp, Mediterranean flavors come together in this salad. The dressing can be thickened to make a great dip for pita chips or veggies, just add another 2 tablespoons garbanzo bean flour prior to cooking. Hummus dip or dressing can take on many flavors. Try adding 2 tablespoons pesto, roasted red peppers or sun-dried tomatoes.

- 6 cups salad greens
- 1 cup kalamata olives
- 1/2 red onion, thinly sliced
- 1 cucumber, sliced
- 1/2 cup roasted red peppers, sliced
- 1 cup feta cheese
- 1/2 cup fresh parsley leaves

Hummus Dressing:
- 1 1/2 cups water
- 1/3 cup garbanzo bean flour
- 2 cloves garlic, minced
- 2 tablespoons tahini paste
- 1 teaspoon salt
- 1/2 teaspoon cumin
- 1/4 teaspoon cayenne pepper
- 2-3 tablespoons lemon juice
- 2 tablespoons olive oil

In a small saucepan, whisk bean flour into water. Bring to a low boil. Lower heat and simmer 10-15 minutes, stirring often. Remove bean mixture from heat and cool completely. Divide salad ingredients on 4-8 plates (depending on serving size). Add additional ingredients to dressing, stirring until combined. Add additional water and salt if needed. Refrigerate until ready to serve.

Hideaway Bread Salad

The secret to this salad is in making the croutons. Make extra, as they are so good they may get nibbled away before the salad gets put together. Any bread can be used, in fact this salad is made more colorful by adding more than one kind.

Croutons:
- 6 cups Hideaway Bread, cubed (see page 49) or any day-old artisan bread
- 2-4 tablespoons olive oil
- Garlic powder
- Salt

- 1 cup onion, thinly sliced
- 1/4 cup extra-virgin olive oil
- 2 tablespoons wine vinegar
- 1-2 tablespoons fresh basil and/or parsley
- 4 tomatoes, chopped

In a large skillet, heat about 1/4" olive oil. Add croutons and toss gently to coat with oil. (This may need to be done in a few batches). Sprinkle with garlic powder and salt. Sauté until golden brown, transfer to a baking sheet. Bake croutons at 350° until crunchy, stirring frequently, about 5-7 minutes. Cool croutons. In a large bowl mix salad ingredients, adding tomatoes and croutons last. Toss gently and serve immediately.

- 2/3 cup kamut® flour
- 2/3 cup whole wheat flour
- 2/3 cup almond meal/flour
- 1/2 teaspoon salt
- 2 eggs
- 2 teaspoons extra-virgin olive oil

In a medium bowl, mix dry ingredients until thoroughly combined. Add eggs and oil. Mix dough until a ball is formed. Place on a lightly floured surface and knead 5-7 minutes. Roll out to 1/4" and cut long noodles to 1/4". To cook pasta, boil water in a large stock pot. Add pasta and cook 3-4 minutes. Gently remove pasta from water, season with butter, extra-virgin olive oil or your favorite sauce and serve immediately.

Not only is this a nutrition-packed pasta, it's fun to make. Kids especially enjoy rolling out the dough and cutting it with a pizza cutter. Since it cooks up so fast it is instant gratification for budding chefs.

Green Pea Pasta

This is one of those recipes that has to be tried to believe how great it tastes. Depending on the size of the pasta it can have a delicate texture or, if made into thicker noodles, can resemble a dumpling.

- 1 1/2 cups whole wheat or spelt flour
- 1/2 cup green pea flour
- 1/2 teaspoon salt
- 1/4 teaspoon white pepper
- 2 eggs

In a medium bowl, mix dry ingredients until thoroughly combined. Add eggs and mix thoroughly. Run through a pasta machine on desired setting (add a small amount of water if necessary). If hand-making the pasta, mix dough until a ball is formed. Place on a lightly floured surface and knead 5-7 minutes. Roll out to 1/4" and cut into desired shapes. To cook pasta, boil water in a large stock pot. Add pasta and cook 3-4 minutes. Gently remove pasta from water, season with butter, extra-virgin olive oil or your favorite sauce and serve immediately.

Lycopene Pizza-Pasta

- 1 cup whole wheat or spelt flour
- 1 cup triticale flour
- 2 teaspoons Italian seasoning
- 1/2 teaspoon onion powder
- 1/2 teaspoon garlic powder
- 1/2 teaspoon salt
- 2 eggs
- 4-6 tablespoons tomato paste

In a medium bowl, mix dry ingredients until thoroughly combined. Add eggs and tomato paste. Mix dough and run through a pasta machine on desired setting. If hand-making the pasta, cut down on the tomato paste and mix dough until a ball is formed. Place on a lightly floured surface and knead 5-7 minutes. Roll out to 1/4" and cut into desired shapes. To cook pasta, boil water in a large stock pot. Add pasta and cook 3-4 minutes. Gently remove pasta from water, season with butter, extra-virgin olive oil or your favorite sauce and serve immediately.

When my son Kazden was four, he decided that he didn't like anything with too much tomato sauce. I always told him how good tomatoes were because they were full of lycopene. From then on he just called it lycopene and he would actually ask at the pizza parlor if they could go light on the lycopene (this of course usually required a long explanation). A few years later he has grown to like tomato-based things but the antioxidant nickname has stuck.

Breads

GOOD CARBOHYDRATES ARE NOT WORTH GIVING UP. IF YOU CAN GIVE UP ALL THE EMPTY-CALORIE, WHITE PRODUCTS IN YOUR DAILY DIET, THERE WILL BE PLENTY OF ROOM FOR THESE BREADS THAT ARE PACKED WITH NUTRIENTS.

MANY PEOPLE SAY THEY DON'T HAVE TIME TO BAKE. WHEN I LOOK AT THE COST OF BREAD, SPECIFICALLY THE HEALTHY, WHOLE-GRAIN TYPES, I HAVE SEEN IT GO FOR AS MUCH AS $7.00 A LOAF. AT THAT PRICE, I FIND TIME TO BAKE.

DON'T BE INTIMIDATED BY BREAD BAKING. MAKE IT EASY AND TRY A MACHINE; GET A WAFFLE MAKER, SOME MUFFIN TINS, OR A TORTILLA PRESS. NUTRITIOUS FLOURS GO WITH BREAD LIKE SALT GOES WITH PEPPER. THINK ABOUT THE EASY SUBSTITUTIONS — INSTEAD OF A QUICK, LOW-FIBER WHITE PASTA, IT TAKES ABOUT THE SAME AMOUNT OF TIME TO PUT TOGETHER A NUTRITIOUS, QUICK BREAD AS A DINNER SIDE FULL OF COMPLEX CARBOHYDRATES.

Confetti Bread

A wonderful way to get four cups of vegetables in a single batch of bread. It is so good it can be made in a cake pan and served for dessert – don't forget the cream cheese frosting. Depending on the bounty of my garden I have made this bread with only one of the veggies or a combination that totals 4 cups.

- 1 1/2 cups oil
- 2 cups sugar
- 4 eggs
- 1 cup grated carrots
- 2 teaspoons vanilla
- 1/2 cup dried cherries or cranberries
- 1 cup grated zucchini
- 1 cup grated yellow summer squash
- 1 cup rhubarb, diced
- 2 cups whole wheat or spelt flour
- 1 cup kamut® flour
- 1 cup sorghum or brown rice flour
- 1/2 cup almond or hazelnut meal/flour
- 5 teaspoons cinnamon
- 2 teaspoons baking soda
- 1 teaspoon baking powder
- 1 teaspoon salt

Preheat oven to 325°. In a large bowl cream oil and sugar. Add eggs and vanilla and beat until smooth. Add vegetables and dried fruit and mix well. Sift remaining ingredients into mixing bowl and mix until thoroughly combined. Do not overmix. Divide batter into three greased loaf pans. Bake 45-55 minutes or until bread tests done. (A 9" by 13" pan can also be used, decrease baking time by 10 minutes.)

Autumn Harvest Muffins

- 1 cup oil
- 1 1/2 cups sugar
- 3 eggs
- 1/2 cup milk
- 2 teaspoons vanilla
- 2 cups pumpkin puree
- 1 1/2 cups whole wheat or spelt flour
- 1/2 cup quinoa flour
- 1/2 cup amaranth flour
- 1/2 cup toasted wheat germ
- 1 teaspoon baking soda
- 1 teaspoon salt
- 1/2 teaspoon baking powder
- 3 teaspoons pumpkin pie spice or cinnamon
- 1/2-1 cup chopped nuts and/or raisins (optional)

Preheat oven to 400°. In a medium bowl cream oil and sugar. Add eggs and beat until smooth. Add milk, vanilla and pumpkin, mixing well. Sift remaining dry ingredients into mixing bowl and mix until thoroughly combined. Do not overmix. Fold in nuts and/or raisins. Scoop batter into greased muffin tins or mini-loaf pans. Bake 10-12 minutes for mini-muffins, 18-20 for standard muffins and 25-30 for mini-loaf pans.

Something about the fall season starts my craving for all things pumpkin. These soft, delicate muffins are a powerhouse of nutrition. They are very versatile in that they can be made into any size: muffin, loaf or cake. Many times I make a combination of several shapes. Just note that different size pans require different baking times.

Backpacker Bites

Specifically developed for my husband's trekking trips into the wilderness, I figured if he only ate these for three days, he would still feel great. He loved them, so now, along with a few bacon and peanut butter sandwiches, dried apples, and a good supply of Power Balls (pg. 84), he is good to go for a week.

- 1 cup brown sugar
- 3/4 cup canola oil
- 3 eggs
- 3 teaspoons vanilla
- 6 ripe bananas, mashed
- 1/2 cup buttermilk or plain yogurt
- 1 cup whole wheat or spelt flour
- 2/3 cup soy flour
- 2/3 cup wheat germ
- 1 cup wheat bran
- 1/2 cup garbanzo bean flour
- 1/2 cup quinoa flour
- 1 teaspoon baking soda
- 1 teaspoon baking powder
- 1 teaspoon salt
- 1 tablespoon cinnamon

Preheat oven to 400°. In a large bowl cream oil and sugar. Add eggs and vanilla and beat until smooth. Add buttermilk and bananas and mix well. Sift dry ingredients into mixing bowl and mix until thoroughly combined. Do not overmix. Scoop batter into greased muffin tins or mini-loaf or donut pans. Bake 10 minutes for mini-muffins, 16-18 for standard muffins and 20-25 for mini-loaf pans.

Ginger Powered Muffins

- 2/3 cup olive oil
- 2/3 cup brown sugar or 1/2 cup honey
- 3 eggs
- 1 cup cooked sweet potatoes, pureed
- 1/3 cup plain yogurt or sour cream
- 1 cup whole wheat or spelt flour
- 1/2 cup teff flour
- 1/2 cup quinoa flour
- 1/2 cup wheat germ or flax meal
- 2 teaspoons ginger
- 1 teaspoon baking soda
- 1/2 teaspoon baking powder
- 1/4 teaspoon salt

Preheat oven to 350°. In a medium bowl cream oil and sugar or honey. Add eggs and beat until smooth. Add sweet potatoes and yogurt and mix well. Sift dry ingredients into mixing bowl and mix until thoroughly combined. Do not overmix. Scoop batter into greased muffin tins or mini-loaf pans. Bake 20-25 minutes or until muffins test done.

Because of their tremendous anti-inflammatory properties, both sweet potatoes and ginger are a great addition to a healthy diet. I like to bake up large batches of sweet potatoes, puree them and add them to other breads, cakes, and cookies as well. I've even snuck them into macaroni and cheese and people had no idea!

Roadside Rhubarb Bread

Growing up we had a huge rhubarb plant that grew in the gravel on the side of our driveway. I used to think anything that grew from the rocks couldn't be that good – my mom proved me wrong with amazing strawberry-rhubarb pies. Recently #1 on a super foods list, rhubarb is high in potassium, vitamin C, and fiber along with other nutrients. I enjoy baking with it for its great tart flavor and the moistness it lends to this bread. If you are short on rhubarb substitute bananas, apples, or zucchini.

- 1 1/2 cups brown sugar
- 2/3 cup canola oil
- 1 egg
- 1 teaspoon vanilla or almond extract
- 1 cup plain yogurt
- 1 cup whole wheat flour
- 1 cup spelt flour
- 1/2 cup triticale flour
- 1 teaspoon baking soda
- 1 teaspoon salt
- 2 1/2 cup rhubarb, chopped
- 1/2 cup walnuts or pecans, chopped

Preheat oven to 350°. In a medium bowl cream oil and sugar. Add egg and vanilla or almond extract, and beat until smooth. Add yogurt and mix well. Sift flours, baking soda, and salt into mixing bowl and mix until thoroughly combined. Do not overmix. Fold in rhubarb and nuts. Divide batter into two greased loaf pans. Bake 40-50 minutes or until bread tests done. (A 9" by 13" pan can also be used, bake 35-40 minutes.)

Cheesy Drops

Biscuits are a great addition to lunch or dinner. These flavorful cheese biscuits beg to be dipped in favorite soups and stews. Leftover, they make great little sandwiches for boxed lunches.

- 1 cup whole wheat or spelt flour
- 1 cup kamut® flour
- 4 teaspoons baking powder
- 1/2 teaspoon soda
- 1 teaspoon salt
- 1/3 cup butter
- 2 tablespoons chives or scallions, chopped
- 1/3 cup feta, goat, or blue cheese, crumbled
- 1/3 cup parmesan or romano cheese, grated
- 1 cup buttermilk or plain yogurt

Melted butter for brushing
Parmesan cheese for sprinkling

Preheat oven to 400°. In a large bowl, mix all dry ingredients. Cut butter into dry ingredients until it looks like fine crumbs. Stir in chives and cheeses. Add buttermilk or yogurt, mixing until thoroughly combined. Do not overmix. Drop by tablespoons onto a baking sheet. Bake 15-20 minutes. Remove from oven and brush with melted butter and sprinkle with parmesan cheese, if desired.

Rainbow Corn Cakes

Although three types of cornmeal are used in this recipe for the fun effect of tri-colored muffins, using one type of cornmeal will work just as well. I like to multiply dry ingredients by five and have my own mix ready to whip up at a moment's notice. When camping, I add a can of creamed corn to this mix for "camping cornbread."

- 1/2 cup butter, melted
- 2 eggs
- 1 cup buttermilk or plain yogurt
- 3 tablespoons honey
- 1 1/4 cups white whole wheat flour
- 2 teaspoons baking powder
- 1/4 teaspoon baking soda
- 3/4 teaspoon salt

Mix and divide into thirds
Add to each third:
- 1/3 cup blue corn meal
- 1/3 cup yellow corn meal
- 1/3 cup white corn meal

Preheat oven to 400°. In a medium bowl cream wet ingredients. Sift flour, baking powder, soda and salt into mixing bowl and mix until thoroughly combined. Do not overmix. Divide batter into three bowls. Fold a different cornmeal into each bowl. Scoop batter into greased muffin tins or mini-loaf pans. Bake 10-12 minutes for mini-muffins, 16-18 for standard muffins, and 20-25 for mini-loaf pans. Watch muffins closely and remove as soon as they turn golden. Remove from oven and brush with honey butter if desired.

Eat Your Veggies Bread

- 1 1/2 cups whole wheat flour
- 1/2 cup brown rice flour
- 1/4 cup any bean flour
- 1 tablespoon granulated sugar
- 2 teaspoons baking powder
- 1 teaspoon salt
- 1/3 cup zucchini, grated
- 1/3 cup carrots, grated
- 1/3 cup beets, grated
- 1 1/2 cups beer or club soda
- 1/3 cup olive oil

Preheat oven to 350°. Sift dry ingredients into a large mixing bowl. Add vegetables and stir until combined. Make a well in the center and add beer or club soda and oil. Mix until just combined. Do not overmix. Pour batter into a greased loaf pan. Bake 35-40 minutes or until bread tests done. (A 9" round or square pan can also be used, bake 25-30 minutes.)

This bread definitely takes on the flavors of the vegetables inside, so mix and match them to desired taste. For a nice twist try sautéing vegetables in olive oil before adding them to bread.

Churriana Bread

While living in a tiny coastal town in southern Spain, I had the opportunity to help out in a bakery. Every day I picked up a loaf of dark, dense whole grain bread. It was the first time I had buckwheat groats. Since then I have tossed them in soups, salads, cookies and other quick breads. They are just like nuts!

- 1 cup buttermilk
- 1/3 cup pure maple syrup
- 1/4 cup butter, melted
- 2 eggs, beaten
- 1/2 teaspoon salt
- 2 cups whole wheat or spelt flour
- 1 cup buckwheat flour
- 1/2 cup graham flour
- 1/2 cup toasted buckwheat groats
- 2 1/2 teaspoons yeast

Using a stand mixer or food processor, dissolve yeast in 1 tablespoon warm (105°-110°) water and let sit 5 minutes or until yeast begins to bubble. Add wet ingredients and mix thoroughly. In a separate bowl mix all dry ingredients. Add to mixer or processor and beat or pulse until dough is smooth and pulls away from the sides of the bowl. Remove dough hook or blade, cover and let dough rise until doubled, about an hour. Punch down dough, form into desired shape and let rise a second time, 30 minutes to 1 hour. Bake in a preheated 350° oven 35-45 minutes or until bread is golden and sounds hollow when tapped. Bread is also done when an instant-read thermometer reads 195°-200°.

For dough in the bread machine, add ingredients in the order they are listed and press the dough cycle. For a cooked loaf, follow directions on the machine for light crust, whole wheat bread.

Happy Hybrid Bread

- 1 cup milk
- 1/4 cups warm water (105°-110°)
- 2 tablespoons butter, melted
- 2 tablespoons canola or light olive oil
- 1 egg
- 1 tablespoon honey
- 1 teaspoon salt
- 1/3 cup dry milk
- 2 3/4 cups triticale flour
- 2 teaspoons yeast

Using a stand mixer or food processor, dissolve yeast in warm water, let sit 5 minutes or until yeast begins to bubble. Add wet ingredients and mix thoroughly. In a separate bowl mix all dry ingredients. Add to mixer or processor and beat or pulse until dough is smooth and pulls away from the sides of the bowl. Remove dough hook or blade, cover and let dough rise until doubled, about an hour. Punch down dough, form into desired shape and let rise a second time, 30 minutes to 1 hour. Bake in a preheated 350° oven 25-30 minutes or until bread is golden and sounds hollow when tapped. Bread is also done when an instant-read thermometer reads 195°-200°.

For dough in the bread machine, add ingredients in the order they are listed and press the dough cycle. For a cooked loaf, press follow directions on the machine for light crust whole wheat bread.

Triticale flour is a wheat and rye hybrid. It makes a nice bread that resembles whole wheat with just a hint of rye. And using hybrid things is so politically correct these days, isn't it?

Whole, Dark & Handsome

*R*eminiscent of something one might find in a European village, this bread is packed with vital nutrients. As dark as it is, it has a surprisingly light crumb to it. Spread with sweet cream butter, it's wonderful served right out of the oven.

- 1 cup warm water (105°-110°)
- 1/4 cup molasses
- 1/4 cup butter, melted
- 1 teaspoon salt
- 1 cup rye flour
- 1/2 cup buckwheat flour
- 1/3 cup cocoa powder
- 1 3/4 cups whole wheat or spelt flour
- 2 teaspoons yeast

Using a stand mixer or food processor, dissolve yeast in warm water, let sit 5 minutes or until yeast begins to bubble. Add molasses and butter and mix thoroughly. In a separate bowl mix all dry ingredients. Add to mixer or processor and beat or pulse until dough is smooth and pulls away from the sides of the bowl. Remove dough hook or blade, cover and let dough rise until doubled, about an hour. Punch down dough, form into desired shape. (This bread bakes nicely as a freeform round loaf on a pizza stone.) Let rise a second time, 30 minutes to 1 hour. Bake in a preheated 400° oven 25-30 minutes or until bread is golden and sounds hollow when tapped. Bread is also done when an instant-read thermometer reads 195°-200°.

For dough in the bread machine, add ingredients in the order they are listed and press the dough cycle. For a cooked loaf, follow directions on the machine for light crust, whole wheat bread.

Hideaway Bread

- 1 cup buttermilk
- 1/4 cup warm water (105°-110°)
- 1 tablespoon maple syrup
- 1 tablespoon olive oil
- 1 1/2 teaspoons salt
- 1 teaspoon lemon zest
- 1 teaspoon garlic powder
- 3/4 cup rye flour
- 2 cups whole wheat pastry flour
- 2 teaspoons yeast

Although developed for the Hideaway Bread Salad, this bread has a wonderful savory flavor and makes a great accompaniment to any Italian cuisine. It also makes great garlic bread or rolls.

Using a stand mixer or food processor, dissolve yeast in warm water, let sit 5 minutes or until yeast begins to bubble. Add buttermilk, maple syrup and olive oil, mixing thoroughly. In a separate bowl mix all dry ingredients. Add to mixer or processor and beat or pulse until dough is smooth and pulls away from the sides of the bowl. Remove dough hook or blade, cover and let dough rise until doubled, about an hour. Punch down dough, form into desired shape and let rise a second time, 30 minutes to 1 hour. Bake in a preheated 350° oven 25-30 minutes or until bread is golden and sounds hollow when tapped. Bread is also done when an instant-read thermometer reads 195°-200°.

For dough in the bread machine, add ingredients in the order they are listed and press the dough cycle. For a cooked loaf press follow directions on the machine for light crust whole wheat bread.

Not-For-The-Birds

*B*lessed with a husband who will try anything I cook, he thought I had lost my mind when I served him millet for the first time. "Did you get this out of the bird feeder?" was his first question. Realizing much of the world's population has been enjoying millet for centuries, has opened our minds to millet. By the way, my husband loves the flavor of this bread!

- 1 cup warm water (105°-110°)
- 2 teaspoons sugar
- 1/2 cup milk
- 2 tablespoons light olive oil
- 1 teaspoon salt
- 1 1/2 cups whole wheat or spelt flour
- 3/4 cup quinoa, triticale flour or pastry flour
- 3/4 cup millet flour
- 2 tablespoons corn meal
- 2 tablespoons sesame seeds
- 2 tablespoons sunflower seeds
- 2 teaspoons yeast

Topping:
1 egg white, beaten
1 tablespoon poppy seeds
1 tablespoon millet

Using a stand mixer or food processor, proof yeast in warm water by dissolving sugar in water and sprinkling yeast on top, let sit 10 minutes or until yeast begins to bubble. Add milk and olive oil and mix thoroughly. In a separate bowl mix all dry ingredients. Add to mixer or processor and beat or pulse until dough is smooth and pulls away from the sides of the bowl. Remove dough hook or blade, cover and let dough rise until doubled, about an hour. Punch down dough, form into desired shape. (This bread bakes nicely as a freeform round loaf on a pizza stone.) Let rise a second time, 30 minutes to 1 hour. Brush with egg white and coat with poppy seeds and millet. Bake in a preheated 475° oven 25-30 minutes or until bread is golden and sounds hollow when tapped. Bread is also done when an instant-read thermometer reads 195°-200°.

For dough in the bread machine, add ingredients in the order they are listed and press the dough cycle. For a cooked loaf, follow directions on the machine for light crust whole wheat bread; millet and poppy seeds can be added while bread is mixing.

Olive You Bread

My boys still love this knock-knock joke.

"Knock Knock"
"Who's there?"
"Olive"
"Olive who?"
"Olive-you"

... but it sounds like "I love you!"

- 1 cup warm water (105°-110°)
- 1 1/2 cups mashed potatoes
- 2 tablespoons olive oil
- 2 cups whole wheat pastry flour
- 1/2 cup kamut® flour
- 1/2 cup triticale flour
- 1 teaspoon salt
- 1 1/2 teaspoons yeast
- 1/2 cup Kalamata olives, halved

Using a stand mixer or food processor, dissolve yeast in warm water, let sit 5 minutes or until yeast begins to bubble. Add mashed potatoes and oil and mix thoroughly. In a separate bowl mix all dry ingredients. Add to mixer or processor and beat or pulse until dough is smooth and pulls away from the sides of the bowl. Remove dough hook or blade, cover and let dough rise until doubled, about an hour. Punch down dough, shape into a flat round circle about 1" high. Press olives evenly into dough and let rise a second time, 30 minutes to 1 hour. Bake in a preheated 400° oven 25-30 minutes or until bread is golden and sounds hollow when tapped. Bread is also done when an instant-read thermometer reads 195°-200°.

For dough in the bread machine, add ingredients in the order they are listed and press the dough cycle. When complete, shape into a flat round circle and follow recipe instructions.

- 1 cup warm water (105°-110°)
- 1 tablespoon sugar
- 2 teaspoons yeast
- 1 tablespoon olive oil
- 2/3 cups millet flour
- 1/2 cup sorghum flour
- 1/3 cup cornstarch
- 1/2 cup potato starch
- 1 teaspoon guar gum
- 1 teaspoon salt

Using a hand or stand mixer, proof yeast in warm water by dissolving sugar in water and sprinkling yeast on top, let sit 10 minutes or until yeast begins to bubble. Add oil to yeast mixture. In a separate bowl whisk dry ingredients until fully combined. Add dry ingredients to mixer and beat at high speed 3-4 minutes. Spoon into a greased loaf pan and let rise until doubled, about 1 hour. Bake in a preheated 375° oven 30-40 minutes or until bread is golden and sounds hollow when tapped. Bread is also done when an instant-read thermometer reads 195°-200°. Cool at least 15 minutes before slicing.

So many times I have been disappointed with tasteless gluten-free products purchased, ready made. Although this recipe does require a little shopping, it is well worth the effort. While the ingredients are out, try mixing up the dry ingredients for several batches. I keep them in labeled, sealable plastic bags with directions on what liquid ingredients to add when I am ready to bake.

Tomorrow Bread

This kid-friendly recipe is a great way to introduce children to bread baking and nutritious flours. It is an easy one to measure and makes for a good counting lesson. My kids named it Tomorrow Bread because it is mixed today and baked tomorrow.

- 1 cup kamut® flour
- 1 cup triticale flour
- 1 cup unbleached white flour
- 1 teaspoon salt
- 1/2 teaspoon yeast
- 1 3/4 cup warm water (105°)

In a large bowl, mix flours, salt and yeast until thoroughly combined. Add water and mix until all flour is moistened. Cover with plastic wrap and let sit 10-20 hours on the counter. Place a clean dish towel on the counter. Sprinkle a generous amount of white flour on the towel. Using a rubber scraper, scrape bread dough on to floured towel. Fold dough in on itself so it forms a ball. Let rise 1-2 hours or until double in size. Preheat the oven and a cast iron skillet or pizza stone to 400°. Gently roll dough onto hot pan or pizza stone. Cover with foil and bake 30 minutes. Remove foil for the last 5-10 minutes. Enjoy warm with butter, honey and jam.

Flat's Where It's At

*F*lat breads are fun because they can be any size and shape you desire. These puff up and can also be split open and used as pitas. Brush with butter and sprinkle with cinnamon and sugar for a sweet variation.

- 2 cups warm water (105°-110°)
- 1 1/2 teaspoons dry yeast
- 1 tablespoon sugar
- 2 cups whole wheat or spelt flour
- 1 cup rye flour
- 1/2 cup sorghum flour
- 1/4 cup garbanzo bean flour
- 1 tablespoon salt

Using a stand mixer or food processor, proof yeast in warm water by dissolving sugar in water and sprinkling yeast on top, let sit 10 minutes or until yeast begins to bubble. Add whole wheat or spelt flour and beat one minute. Let sit 20-30 minutes. Sift remaining ingredients into mixer or processor and beat or pulse until dough is smooth and pulls away from the sides of the bowl. Form dough into 10-15 balls. On a lightly floured surface, roll balls to 1/3". Place on baking sheets and let sit 20 minutes. Bake in a preheated 400° oven 6-8 minutes or until golden brown. Brush with garlic butter and serve warm.

Newlywed Rolls

- 1 1/4 cups warm water (105°-110°)
- 2 1/2 teaspoons active dry yeast
- 1/4 cup sugar
- 1/2 cup canola oil
- 2 eggs
- 2 cups whole wheat or spelt flour
- 1/2 cup brown rice or millet flour
- 1/2 cup kamut® or quinoa flour
- 1 teaspoon salt

In a large bowl, proof yeast in warm water by dissolving sugar in water and sprinkling yeast on top, let sit 10 minutes or until yeast begins to bubble. Add oil and eggs and beat until smooth. Add flours and salt to ingredients and beat with a hand mixer or whisk 2-3 minutes. Spoon into greased muffin tins and let rise 30-40 minutes. Bake in a preheated 350° oven 18-20 minutes or until golden brown.

Less than a month married, these rolls were part of the first dinner I made for my husband. Of course the eggs were powdered but Scott didn't mind. They quickly became a regular addition to our table and I think I did get to his heart through his stomach with these. Today, 18 years later, he still enjoys these rolls.

Funky Monkey

ased on a decadent sticky bun bread recipe, I reworked this one to at least provide some fiber benefits. It can be pulled apart like a sticky bun or cut with a very sharp knife and served in slices.

- 1 1/4 cup warm water (105°-110°)
- 2 tablespoons brown sugar
- 2 tablespoons butter, melted
- 1 egg
- 2 cups spelt or whole wheat flour
- 1 1/2 cups kamut® or triticale flour
- 1 teaspoon salt
- 1 tablespoon dry yeast

For rolling:
- 1 3.5-ounce box cook and serve butterscotch pudding
- 1/4 cup flax meal
- 6 tablespoons butter, melted
- 1/3 cup honey

Using a stand mixer or food processor, proof yeast in warm water by dissolving brown sugar in water and sprinkling yeast on top, let sit 10 minutes or until yeast begins to bubble. Add butter and egg and mix thoroughly. Add flours and salt to mixer or processor and beat or pulse until dough is smooth and pulls away from the sides of the bowl. Remove dough hook or blade, cover and let dough rise until doubled, about an hour. Punch down dough, divide into 15-20 balls. In a small bowl mix melted butter and honey and in a second bowl, mix pudding and flax meal. Grease a bundt or tube pan. Take each ball and roll it in the honey butter, then coat with the dry pudding mixture. Place in the pan. Repeat until all balls are coated and in the pan. Pour any remaining butter and/or pudding over the pan. Let rise an additional 30-40 minutes. Bake in a preheated 350° oven 25-35 minutes or until bread is golden and sounds hollow when tapped. Bread is also done when an instant-read thermometer reads 195°-200°.

For dough in the bread machine, add ingredients in the order they are listed and press the dough cycle. When complete divide dough into 15-20 balls and follow steps outlined in the recipe.

Outside-In Pizza

Like a mini-calzone, these can be stuffed with just about anything. Double or triple the batch and have an Outside-In Pizza Bar Party where guests can choose from several different fillings. Use toothpicks to poke vent holes in letter shapes to identify whose pizza is whose. Dough and toppings can also be used for pizza prepared in the traditional fashion.

Dough:
- 1 1/2 cups warm water (105°-110°)
- 1 teaspoon sugar
- 2 tablespoons extra virgin olive oil
- 1 1/2 cups kamut® flour
- 1 cup whole wheat pastry flour
- 1 tablespoon corn meal
- 1 1/2 teaspoons salt
- 2 1/2 teaspoons dry yeast

Filling Suggestions:
- Marinara Sauce
- Pesto Sauce
- Creamy Garlic Dressing
- Assorted Grated Cheeses
- Diced mushrooms, olives, peppers, onions, tomatoes or pineapple
- Diced cooked chicken, pepperoni, ham or tempe

Using a stand mixer or food processor, proof yeast in warm water by dissolving sugar in water and sprinkling yeast on top, let sit 10 minutes or until yeast begins to bubble. Add oil and mix thoroughly. Add flours, cornmeal and salt to mixer or processor and beat or pulse until dough is smooth and pulls away from the sides of the bowl. Remove dough hook or blade, cover and let dough rise until doubled, about an hour. Punch down dough, divide into 4 balls. On a lightly floured surface, roll balls to 1/3". Fill half of the circle with desired fillings. Fold over and seal edges. Make a few slits in the top and let sit 10 minutes. Bake in a preheated 400° oven 25-30 minutes or until bread is golden.

For dough in the bread machine, add ingredients in the order they are listed and press the dough cycle. When complete, divide dough into 4 balls and follow steps outlined in the recipe.

Mas Tortillas Por Favor

*T*he first time I ever made tortillas I had a hard time getting it right. We lived in the Alaskan bush, where we were teaching school. Every flop I had went out the window. One of our students happened to be driving by on a snow mobile when he got hit with one (we were living in 24 hours of darkness at the time.) He picked it up and ate it. Before long I had a line of snow mobiles at my window and I was handing out tortillas to kids as fast as I could make them. A few dozen tortillas later, I got pretty good at the technique.

Black Bean Tortillas:
- 2 cups whole wheat or spelt flour
- 1/2 cup black bean flour
- 1/2 teaspoon salt
- 1/3 cup canola oil
- 1 cup warm water

Gluten-Free Tortillas:
- 2 cups quinoa flour
- 1/2 teaspoon salt
- 1/4 cup canola oil
- 2/3 cup warm water

Combination Tortillas:
- 1 cup kamut® flour
- 1 cup triticale flour
- 1/2 teaspoon salt
- 1/4 cup canola oil
- 2/3 cup warm water

In a medium bowl, mix flours and salt. Blend in oil with a fork or pastry cutter. Gradually add water to form a ball of dough that just holds together. Divide dough into 10-15 equal balls. Cover with plastic wrap and let sit 30 minutes. Use a floured tortilla press or rolling pin and flatten to 1/8" on a lightly floured surface. Cook on a hot, nonstick or cast iron skillet until tortilla begins to brown and crisp, flip frequently. Serve as a soft taco shell, roll for a burrito or enchilada or butter and top with jam or honey for a sweet treat.

'LOVE'ly Waffles

*W*affles used to be a special breakfast at my house but when I realized how easy they were with almost no cleanup, we started having them more often. These waffles pack an added protein boost from the nut flour. For the easiest cleanup make sure you get a good nonstick waffle iron.

- 2 eggs
- 3 cups milk
- 3 tablespoons olive or canola oil
- 1 cup triticale or kamut® flour
- 1 cup whole wheat or spelt flour
- 2 tablespoons brown sugar
- 2 teaspoons cinnamon
- 2 teaspoons baking powder
- 1/2 teaspoon salt
- 1 cup hazelnut or almond meal/flour

In a medium bowl, whisk wet ingredients until frothy. Sift in dry ingredients and mix until combined. Fold in nut flour. Do not overmix. Using a ladle, spoon onto preheated waffle iron. Follow manufacturer's directions, baking until golden brown. (My new waffle iron has several settings, similar to a toaster. It actually beeps when the waffles are ready.)

Pancake Day Banana Pancakes

- 2 cups milk
- 1 tablespoon lemon juice
- 2 tablespoons sugar
- 1 tablespoon canola oil
- 1-2 eggs
- 1 1/2 cups whole wheat or spelt flour
- 1/2 cup brown rice or soy flour
- 2 teaspoons baking powder
- 1/2 teaspoon baking soda
- 1/2 teaspoon salt
- 1-2 bananas, thinly sliced or 1 cup blueberries or chocolate chips

In a medium bowl, whisk wet ingredients until frothy. Sift in dry ingredients and mix until combined. Do not overmix. Using a ladle, spoon out about 1/4 cup pancake mixture onto a hot, well-greased or nonstick griddle. Quickly place banana slices or blueberries or chocolate chips on the top of the pancake. Once pancake begins to bubble it is ready to flip. Flip pancake and cook until lightly golden. Serve with butter, syrup and whipped cream if desired.

While living in Indonesia we adhered to a regular breakfast schedule. Fridays were always a little sweeter because it was always pancake day. A specialty of our ibu was banana pancakes. Every time I eat them I have memories of dining on the porch while watching the monkeys feast out of the mango tree in our yard.

Wheat-Free All-Week Pancake Mix

I don't know about your sometimes picky kids, or grand-kids or husbands or wives, but I do know that my picky boys will eat almost anything as long as it is in pancake form. Pancakes have actually been the best way for me to recipe test the flavors of all of the flours. Because you don't need to rely on gluten you can experiment away with this bread style. This is a quadruple batch so it should last most of the week for 3-4 people.

- 1 cup spelt flour
- 1 cup quinoa or kamut® flour
- 1 cup sorghum or millet flour
- 1 cup oat or barley flour
- 1/2 cup teff or buckwheat flour
- 1/4 cup sugar
- 1/4 cup baking powder
- 1 teaspoon salt

In a large bowl, add dry mix ingredients and whisk until thoroughly combined. Store in an airtight container.

To each heaping cup of mix, add:
- 1-2 eggs
- 3/4 cup milk or water
- 1 tablespoon light olive or canola oil

Follow pancake cooking instructions outlined in Pancake Day Pancakes (page 65). For a variation try some last-minute add-ins such as 1/3 cup pureed squash, pumpkin, sweet potato, banana or pureed cottage cheese. Pancakes will be a bit more fragile so take care when flipping.

Anything In A Blanket

- 1 1/4 cup warm milk (105°)
- 1 1/2 teaspoon yeast
- 1/2 cup whole wheat flour
- 3/4 cup buckwheat or teff flour
- 1/2 teaspoon salt
- 2 eggs, beaten
- 3 tablespoons butter, melted
- 2 tablespoons sour cream or plain yogurt

In a medium bowl, add yeast to warm milk, stir until dissolved. Add flours and beat until smooth. Let sit 30 minutes. Add salt, butter, eggs and sour cream. Stir until combined. Do not overmix. Using a ladle, spoon out about 2-3 tablespoons pancake mixture onto a hot, well-greased or nonstick griddle. Once pancake begins to bubble it is ready to flip. Flip pancake and cook until lightly golden. Serve with your favorite filling.

Whether it's goat cheese, chives and smoked salmon, or fresh raspberries and sweetened whip cream, anything wrapped in these buckwheat pancakes is a special treat and a great introduction to buckwheat or teff. Move over Pigs-In-A-Blanket, we've got blinis!

African Pancakes

One of my favorite flours to use for pancakes is teff. It reminds me of the many wonderful Ethiopian meals I have enjoyed. These pancakes can be served for breakfast or used as the plate, napkin and utensil when cooking east African cuisine.

- 2 cups warm water
- 1 cup teff flour
- 1/2 cup whole wheat or spelt flour
- 1/2 cup sorghum or millet flour
- 1/4 teaspoon salt
- 1/4 teaspoon yeast

In a medium bowl, mix 1 cup water with 1 cup teff flour and yeast. (To make authentically flavored pancakes, ferment this mixture by leaving it on the counter up to 3 days.) Add remaining ingredients and stir until combined. Do not overmix. For pancakes, spoon out about 1/4 cup pancake mixture onto a hot, well-greased or nonstick griddle. For injera-style pancakes, use 1/2-2/3 cup of batter. Once pancake begins to bubble it is ready to flip. Flip pancake and cook until lightly golden.

Potato Pancakes

As much as we love mashed potatoes, there always seems to be a cup or so leftover. These light, fluffy pancakes are a great way to use up the extras. Serve with syrup and jelly or like a traditional lattke with herbed garlic butter.

- 1 cup buttermilk
- 1 cup water
- 2 eggs
- 1 1/2 cups mashed potatoes
- 1 cup brown rice flour
- 1 cup triticale or kamut® flour
- 1 teaspoon baking soda
- 1/4 teaspoon baking powder
- 1/2 teaspoon salt

In a medium bowl, whisk wet ingredients until frothy. Add mashed potatoes and mix well. Sift in dry ingredients and mix until combined. Do not overmix. Using a ladle, spoon out about 2 tablespoons pancake mixture onto a hot, well-greased or nonstick griddle. Once pancake begins to bubble it is ready to flip. Flip pancake and cook until lightly golden.

Herb Butter:
- 3/4 cup fresh parsley, cilantro, basil and/or chives
- 1 clove garlic
- 2 teaspoons lemon juice
- 4 tablespoons butter, softened
- Salt to taste

Wash herbs and roughly chop. In a food processor or mini-chopper, blend all ingredients until thoroughly combined.

Healthy Snacks

Yes, eat between meals. I love snack time as it gives me the opportunity to introduce people to new things. Everyone loves to snack and many times palates tend to be more adventurous when the tummy is hungry. It can be less intimidating to introduce different foods at snack time because we don't have the "finish everything on your plate" mentality that may come with meal time.

Time For Tea Biscuits

L ike a rusk, these high-fiber, whole-grain cookie-like biscuits can be used as a snack with a hot cup of tea or coffee or ice cold milk. Made for dunking or teething small children, these biscuits are also great for care packages.

- 2 cups whole wheat or spelt flour
- 1 cup brown rice flour
- 1/2 cup almond or hazelnut meal/flour
- 1/2 cup oat flour
- 1/3 cup sugar
- 2 teaspoons baking powder
- 1 teaspoon cinnamon
- 1/2 teaspoon salt
- 3/4 cup milk
- 1/2 tablespoon vinegar
- 1/2 cup melted butter
- 2 eggs
- 3 teaspoons vanilla
- 2 teaspoons almond extract

Preheat oven to 400 degrees. In a large mixing bowl, thoroughly mix all dry ingredients. In a small bowl combine milk and vinegar, let sit 1 minute. Add remaining wet ingredients, blending well. Pour wet into the dry ingredients and stir until you have a soft dough, similar to biscuit dough. Turn the dough onto a well-floured surface and roll to 1/2" thick. Using a pizza cutter or sharp knife, cut the dough into desired shapes and sizes. Place on baking sheets and bake for 15 minutes or until biscuits begin to brown. Remove from the oven and turn over. Reduce heat to 200°. Place back in the oven and bake until biscuits are very dry and hard, 3-4 hours.

Snow Scones

- 1/2 cup butter, chilled
- 1/4 cup sugar
- 1 1/2 cups buttermilk or plain yogurt
- 1 cup white whole wheat flour
- 1 cup kamut® flour or whole wheat
- 1 cup coconut flour
- 1 cup quinoa flour
- 1/2 cup brown rice flour
- 1 tablespoon baking powder
- 1 teaspoon baking soda
- 1/2 teaspoon salt
- 3/4 cup white chocolate chips
- 1 cup coconut
- 1 cup macadamia nuts, chopped
- Butter and sugar for brushing and sprinkling

Preheat oven to 400°. In a large bowl, mix all dry ingredients. Cut butter into dry ingredients until it resembles a fine crumb. Add buttermilk or yogurt, mixing until dough forms a ball. On a floured surface, knead dough 30 seconds. Form dough into a log, 1 1/2" high x 5" wide x 18" long. Cut squares, then split the squares into triangles. Brush with melted butter and sprinkle with sugar, if desired. Bake 25-30 minutes.

Scones are very versatile in that ingredients can vary from a few, like in a traditional English scone, to many like this one that uses several nutritious flours and the wonderful flavor combination of white chocolate, coconut, and macadamia nuts.

Blueberry Crumble Cakes

ifferent versions of the blueberry muffin are a staple around our household. Be it pancakes, scones, mini-muffins, or cake, it has been created in my kitchen. We also enjoy plain old frozen blueberries for their incredible nutritional and antioxidant properties.

- 1/2 cup butter, softened
- 3/4 cup sugar
- 2 eggs
- 1 cup whole wheat flour
- 3/4 cup coconut flour
- 1 teaspoons baking powder
- 1/2 teaspoon salt
- 1/2 teaspoon mace or nutmeg
- 3/4 cup milk
- 1 1/2 cup blueberries

Preheat oven to 350°. In a medium bowl cream butter and sugar. Add eggs and mix until smooth. Add milk and mix well. Sift flours, baking powder, salt and spices into mixing bowl and mix until thoroughly combined. Do not overmix. Fold in fresh or frozen blueberries. Scoop batter into greased muffin tins or mini-loaf pans. Bake 25-30 minutes or until cake tests done.

Black & Blue Biscotti

*O*ne of my favorite snacks to make and eat is biscotti. These crunchy cookies lend themselves to healthy additions like nuts, dried fruits, and nutritious flours. The black bean flour in these gives them an added protein boost.

- 1/2 cup butter
- 3/4 cup sugar
- 3 eggs
- 1 tablespoon vanilla
- 1/2 teaspoon almond flavoring
- 1 tablespoon lemon zest, optional
- 1/2 cup blue corn flour
- 1/2 cup black bean flour
- 1 3/4 cups whole wheat or spelt flour
- 2 teaspoons baking powder
- 1/2 teaspoon salt
- 1/2 cup toasted, chopped nuts, or buckwheat groats

Preheat oven to 350°. In a large bowl, cream first five ingredients. In another bowl combine remaining ingredients, mixing well. Add dry ingredients to wet ingredients, mixing until combined. Shape dough into two long loaves (about 4" x 10") on a baking sheet. Bake 20 minutes. Remove from the oven and slice on the diagonal into 1" slices. Turn slices cut-side down and return to oven, baking an additional 10-15 minutes or until crisp and lightly browned.

Sand Dollars

- 1 cup butter
- 2 eggs
- 2/3 cup brown sugar
- 1 cup buckwheat flour
- 1 cup quinoa flour
- 1/2 teaspoon salt
- 1/2 teaspoon baking powder
- Powdered sugar for sprinkling

Preheat oven to 325°. In a large bowl, cream together first three ingredients. Mix dry ingredients in a separate bowl. Add dry ingredients to wet ingredients and stir until smooth. Drop by rounded teaspoonfuls on a baking sheet. Using a cookie press or the bottom of a small glass, press cookies to 1/3". Bake 15-20 minutes. Sprinkle with powdered sugar if desired.

Nothing short of intriguing, these cookies do resemble something from the beach. If introducing buckwheat for the first time, this is a great recipe to start with. These cookies can also be rolled and wrapped in wax paper. Refrigerate until cold and slice before baking.

Sweet Thins

*M*y oldest son, Braxton, came up with the idea for these cracker-type cookies when I first started this book. He loved the idea of a crunchy, crispy cookie that mom would let him have more than just one of. After several collaborations, we came up with Sweet Thins.

- 1/2 cup butter, melted
- 2 eggs
- 1 cup milk
- 1 cup water
- 1 cup whole wheat or spelt flour
- 1/2 cup kamut® or triticale flour
- 1/2 cup amaranth or quinoa flour
- 1/2 cup wheat germ or oat bran
- 1/4 cup brown sugar
- 1 1/2 teaspoons baking powder
- 1/2 teaspoon baking soda
- 1/2 teaspoon salt
- Cinnamon and sugar for topping

Preheat oven to 375°. In a large bowl, cream together first four ingredients. Mix dry ingredients in a separate bowl. Add dry ingredients to wet ingredients and stir until smooth; batter should be thin. Grease two baking sheets. Pour 1/2 of the batter on one sheet and spread evenly to coat the sheet. Repeat on the other sheet. Bake 10-15 minutes, or until cookies are browned. Remove from the oven and cut to desired shape with a pizza cutter or sharp knife. Return to the oven 3-5 minutes or until cookies reach desired texture.

Cookies For Snack Again!

- 1/2 cup butter
- 1/3 cup canola oil
- 1/2 cup brown sugar
- 1/2 cup white sugar
- 2 eggs
- 1 teaspoon vanilla
- Zest of 1 lemon
- 1 cups whole wheat flour or spelt flour
- 1/2 cup soy flour
- 1 teaspoon baking soda
- 1/2 teaspoon salt
- 1 teaspoon cinnamon
- 2 cups rolled oats, spelt, wheat, or barley
- 1 cup oat bran, wheat bran, or flax meal
- 1/3 cup pecans or walnuts, chopped or ground
- 1/3 cup pumpkin seeds or sunflower seeds, chopped or ground
- 1/2 cup unsweetened coconut
- 1 cup dates, chopped (can substitute with raisins, dried cranberries, or prunes)

Preheat oven to 350°. In a large bowl, cream together first six ingredients. Mix dry ingredients in a separate bowl. Add dry ingredients to wet ingredients and stir until smooth. Add chips or chunks. Do not over stir. Drop by rounded teaspoonfuls on a baking sheet. Bake 8 minutes for a chewy cookie, 10 minutes for a crispy cookie.

If there is one surefire way to trick someone into trying healthy flours and whole grains, it's through the cookie. My kids actually think that you make cookies by dumping in "a little of this, and a little of that." Braxton and Kazden helped come up with this one and they were both pleased.

Chocolate "Guess" Cookies

*O*ne of the most fun recipes to taste-test on people, these chewy, chocolatey, almond and vanilla flavored cookies are always a hit and no one will guess what is in them. Everyone is surprised that not only are healthy flours used, but that bean flour is an ingredient. All bean flours, even if only a few tablespoons are used, will increase protein and fiber of any food.

- 1/2 cup butter
- 1/2 cup coconut or canola oil
- 2/3 cup white sugar
- 2/3 cup brown sugar
- 2 eggs
- 2 teaspoons vanilla
- 1/2 teaspoon almond flavoring
- 1/3 cup cocoa powder
- 1 cup oat bran, flax, or wheat germ
- 1 cup almond meal/flour
- 3/4 cup coconut flour or 1 cup millet or barley flour
- 1/2 cup black or white bean flour
- 1/2 cup whole wheat or spelt flour
- 1 teaspoon soda
- 1 teaspoon salt
- 1/2 cup chocolate chips or chunks

Preheat oven to 350°. In a large bowl, cream together first seven ingredients. Mix dry ingredients in a separate bowl. Add dry ingredients to wet ingredients and stir until smooth. Add chips or chunks. Do not over stir. Drop by rounded teaspoonfuls on a baking sheet. Bake 8 minutes for a chewy cookie, 10 minutes for a crispy cookie.

You Can Never Be Too Thin Or Too Crispy

- 1/4 cup butter or light olive oil
- 1/2 cup sugar
- 1 egg
- 2 teaspoons vanilla
- 1 cup almond or hazelnut meal/flour
- 1 cup whole wheat or spelt flour
- 1/2 teaspoon baking soda
- 1/2 teaspoon salt
- 1/4 teaspoon nutmeg or cardamom
- 1/4 cup dried apricots, chopped
- 1/4 cup dried cherries or cranberries, chopped
- 1/4 cup dates or raisins, chopped

... if you are a cookie that is. Twice-baked is the trick to getting these cracker-type cookies just right. Like biscotti, they lend themselves to a variety of healthy ingredients.

Preheat oven to 300°. In a large bowl, cream together first four ingredients. Mix dry ingredients in a separate bowl. Add dry ingredients to wet ingredients and stir until combined. Add dried fruit. Do not over stir. Spread batter into a large, well-greased loaf pan. Bake 25 minutes or until golden brown. Cool completely. Using a sharp knife, cut 1/4"-1/8" slices and place onto a baking sheet. Bake 10 minutes and turn, bake an additional 5-10 minutes or until cookies are crisp.

Power Balls

The combination of ingredients in these power-packed snacks are endless. For a different flavor, substitute 1/2 cup cocoa powder for the coconut flour. For a sweeter treat, coconut or mini chocolate chips can be added. Kids love to make these and once baked they travel and keep well. My husband loves taking these on his extended outdoor adventures.

- 1 cup honey
- 1 cup nut butter (peanut, cashew, or almond)
- 1 cup powdered milk or whey protein powder
- 1/2 cup coconut flour
- 1/2 cup brown rice flour
- 1/2 cup oat flour
- 1/2 cup rolled oats, spelt, barley, triticale, or wheat
- 1/2 cup wheat germ or flax meal
- 1/2 cup almond or hazelnut meal/flour
- 1/2 cup dried cranberries, chopped
- 1/2 cup raisins, chopped

Using a standing mixer or food processor, combine all ingredients until mixture forms a ball. Form into desired sizes, no larger than 1" in diameter. Roll in almond or hazelnut meal/flour. Power Balls can be eaten as is, making a chewier, stickier treat, or bake 5-6 minutes at 325°.

Sweetie Pie Honey Bunches

his recipe didn't even make it to press before it was handed out to several friends with kids. Not only are these snacks 100% whole grain and healthy, they are an inexpensive alternative to prepackaged snacks.

- 3 cups rolled oats, wheat, barley, triticale, or spelt
- 1 cup coconut (sweetened or unsweetened)
- 1 cup almond or hazelnut meal/flour
- 1/2 cup amaranth or quinoa flour

In a heavy saucepan combine:
- 1 cup butter
- 1 1/2 cups honey
- 1 teaspoon vanilla

In a large mixing bowl mix dry ingredients. In a heavy saucepan, combine butter, honey, and vanilla. Bring mixture to a boil, remove from heat and pour over dry ingredients. Drop by spoonfuls into greased mini-muffin tins. For a crunchy treat bake at 350°, 10 minutes. For a chewy treat, bake at 250°, 20 minutes. These can also be pressed into a greased 9" x 13" pan. Increase baking time 5-10 minutes.

High-Protein Bars

- 1 cup applesauce
- 1/2 cup maple syrup or honey
- 1/4 cup molasses or date syrup
- 2 eggs
- 2 teaspoons vanilla
- 1/3 cup canola oil or light olive oil
- 1 cup wheat germ or oat bran
- 1/2 cup flax meal
- 1 cup ground raw pumpkin or sunflower seeds
- 1 cup powdered milk
- 1/2 cup amaranth flour
- 1/2 cup soy flour
- 1/2 cup brown rice flour
- 2 teaspoons cinnamon
- 1 teaspoon ginger
- 1/2 teaspoon salt

Preheat oven to 325°. In a large bowl, cream together first six ingredients. Mix dry ingredients in a separate bowl. Add dry ingredients to wet ingredients and stir until combined. Press into a greased 9" x 13" pan. Bake 15-20 minutes or until top is no longer sticky. Cool on a wire rack and cut to desired sizes.

To keep these fresh (and to prevent eating the whole batch in one day), these can be cut and wrapped individually in plastic, then frozen. They are perfect for on-the-go snacks and a great addition to boxed breakfasts or lunches.

Go-Go Bars

A fun recipe to name, a friend of mine came to the conclusion that since they are so high in fiber and help keep your energy GOing, they should be dubbed Go-Go Bars. This is another recipe that freezes well in individual servings so it can be "lunch box ready."

- 1/2 cup butter
- 1/2 cup coconut or canola oil
- 3/4 cup brown sugar
- 2 eggs
- 2 teaspoons vanilla
- 2 cups whole wheat or spelt flour
- 1 cup amaranth flour
- 1 cup oat bran, wheat germ or flax meal
- 1 teaspoon soda
- 1/2 teaspoon salt
- 1 cup mini-chocolate chips
- 1 cup coconut or nuts, chopped
- 2/3 cup toasted buckwheat groats

Preheat oven to 350°. In a small bowl soak buckwheat groats in water 5-10 minutes. In a large bowl, cream together first five ingredients. Mix dry ingredients in a separate bowl. Add dry ingredients to wet ingredients and stir until smooth. Drain buckwheat groats, add remaining ingredients and combine. Press into a greased, 9" x 13" pan. Score to desired bar sizes. Bake 20-25 minutes or until top is no longer sticky. Cool on a wire rack and cut to desired sizes.

Dark Bread Crackers

- 1 1/4 cup warm water (105º-110º)
- 2 tablespoons oil
- 2 tablespoons sugar
- 1 cup quinoa flour
- 1 1/2 cups whole wheat or spelt flour
- 1/2 cup teff or buckwheat flour
- 1 teaspoon salt
- 2 1/2 teaspoons yeast

Using a stand mixer or food processor, proof yeast in warm water by dissolving sugar in water and sprinkling yeast on top, let sit 10 minutes or until yeast begins to bubble. In a separate bowl mix all flours and salt. Add to mixer or processor and beat or pulse until dough is smooth and pulls away from the sides of the bowl. Remove dough hook or blade, cover and let dough rise until doubled, about an hour. Punch down dough, shape and place into a greased loaf pan. Let rise a second time, 30 minutes to 1 hour. Bake in a preheated 350º oven 25-30 minutes or until bread is golden and sounds hollow when tapped. Bread is also done when an instant-read thermometer reads 195º-200º.

For dough in the bread machine, add ingredients in the order they are listed and press the dough cycle. For a cooked loaf follow directions on the machine for dark crust whole wheat bread.

To make crackers: Slice bread into bite-sized pieces. Place on a baking sheet and bake in a 375º oven until crisp on the top. Turn pieces over and continue to bake until crisp throughout.

Another recipe rescue idea—when experimenting with breads I found this one far too heavy to eat, as is. Initially I was going to make croutons but I had a party to go to and I was suppose to bring appetizers. The salmon dip was already made so I turned my loaf of bread into crackers. They were a huge hit!

Snacker Crackers

When a tortilla tastes more like a pita style chip than a tortilla, it turns into a Snacker Cracker. Bursting with nutrition, paired with a bean-based dip and summery fruit or veggie salsa, these rank #1 on the healthy snack scale.

- 1 cup whole wheat or spelt flour
- 1/2 cup kamut® flour
- 1/4 cup corn flour
- 1/4 cup brown rice flour
- 4 tablespoons canola or light olive e oil
- 1/2 teaspoon salt
- 3/4 cup warm water

In a medium bowl, mix flours and salt. Blend in oil with a fork or pastry cutter. Gradually add water to form a ball of dough that just holds together. Divide dough into 10-12 equal balls. Cover with plastic wrap and let sit 30 minutes. Use a floured tortilla press or rolling pin and flatten to 1/8" on a lightly floured surface. Cook on a hot, nonstick skillet until tortilla begins to brown and crisp, flip frequently. Cut with a pizza cutter or sharp knife, or tear into serving sizes for a more rustic snack.

Chick Dippers

Many of my extended family members have wheat and gluten allergies. This is one snack everyone can eat and enjoy. Paired with hummus or another bean dip, it makes a very high-protein, high-fiber snack.

- 2 cups garbanzo bean flour
- 1 teaspoon salt
- 2 cups warm water
- 1/4 cup olive oil

In a medium bowl combine all ingredients and whisk until smooth. Let batter sit 30 minutes. Preheat a cast iron skillet or nonstick griddle on medium-high heat. Place a few tablespoons of batter on the pan, lift the pan and tilt so the batter makes a circle. (This is similar to making crepes.) Cook until air bubbles begin to form and bottom begins to brown. Flip and continue cooking until lightly browned. Serve with hummus, baba ghanoush or a favorite chip dip. These can also be rolled with sandwich-type fillings and served as a wrap.

Hummus:
- 1 15-ounce can garbanzo beans, drained
- 3 tablespoons tahini
- 2 cloves garlic
- 1-2 tablespoons water
- 2 tablespoons fresh lemon juice
- 1 tablespoon extra virgin olive oil
- 1/2 teaspoon cumin
- 1/4 cup fresh basil or parsley, optional
- Dash of cayenne or hot pepper sauce

In a food processor or mini-chopper, blend all ingredients until thoroughly combined.

Crispy Critters

It can be a challenge to find a snack that is truly guilt-free. This is one of those rare finds. These crackers stay crisp for several days and satisfy cravings for less healthy chips. Try experimenting with different flavor toppings—the possibilities are endless.

- 1 cup whole wheat or spelt flour
- 1/3 cup teff flour
- 1/3 cup amaranth flour
- 1/3 cup quinoa flour
- 3/4 teaspoon salt
- 1 cup warm water
- 2-3 tablespoons butter, melted
- Parmesan cheese

Preheat oven to 475°. Using a standing mixer or food processor, combine flours, salt, and water until mixture forms a ball. Continue to knead in the mixer 3 minutes or pulse in the processor 1 minute. Remove ball and cover with plastic wrap. Let rest 30 minutes. Divide dough into 3 balls. Place each sheet of dough on its own lightly greased baking sheet. Bake 3-5 minutes or until crackers begin to brown. Remove from the oven and brush with butter and sprinkle with parmesan cheese. Using a pizza cutter or sharp knife, cut to desired shapes and sizes. Return to the oven, baking an additional 3-5 minutes or until crisp.

Desserts

NOT-SO-GUILTY PLEASURES...
HEY, AT LEAST THERE IS
FIBER IN THESE SLIGHTLY
DECADENT TREATS! AND
AREN'T THERE ANTIOXIDANTS
IN CHOCOLATE?!

Crazed Over Coconut Cake

"Where is the whole grain?" is the first question asked when testers tried this cake. The fun thing is how great something can taste while having so much fiber and nutrients. Coconut flour adds a whopping 36 grams of dietary fiber to this recipe. For a great chocolate cake variation substitute 1/4 cup cocoa powder for 1/4 cup of the coconut flour.

- 5 eggs
- 1/2 cup oil
- 1 1/2 cup sugar
- 1/2 cup coconut milk
- 1 teaspoon almond extract
- 3/4 cup coconut flour
- 3/4 cup white whole wheat flour
- 1 teaspoon baking powder
- 1/2 teaspoon salt

Preheat oven to 350°. Using a hand or stand mixer, beat eggs, oil and sugar at high speed 1 minute. Add coconut milk and almond flavoring, stir until combined. Sift dry ingredients into mixing bowl and mix until thoroughly combined. Pour batter into a greased bundt or tube pan. Bake 35-40 minutes or until cake tests done. Let cake cool slightly before icing or glazing.

Amazing Glaze & Topping:
- 2 tablespoons cream cheese
- 2 tablespoons coconut milk
- 2 tablespoons coconut
- 2 tablespoons powdered sugar
- 2/3 cup coconut, toasted (for topping)

Secret P Cake

- 1/2 cup avocado puree or light olive oil
- 1/3 cup butter
- 1 cup sugar
- 4 eggs
- 2 teaspoons vanilla
- 1/2 cup whole wheat or spelt flour
- 1/4 cup green pea flour
- 1 teaspoon baking powder
- 3/4 cup pistachios, ground
- 2/3 cup almond meal/flour

Preheat oven to 325°. Using a hand or stand mixer, beat avocado, butter, and sugar at high speed 1 minute. Add eggs and vanilla, beating an additional minute. Sift flours and baking powder into mixing bowl and mix until thoroughly combined. Fold in pistachios and almond meal/flour. Pour batter into greased 9" round or square cake pan. Bake 45-60 minutes or until cake tests done. Drizzle with sweetened condensed milk and chopped pistachios if desired.

Another one of those recipes that no one will guess the secret ingredients of, this dense, almost chewy cake tastes far more sinful than it actually is. The healthy fat of the avocado combined with nutritious flours makes this one dessert that can have a standing spot in any diet.

Bukittinggi Cake

ased on a deliciously moist, tropical cake we enjoyed at a colorful wedding in Bukittinggi (Bookit-ting-gee) Sumatra, this recipe uses ingredients easily attained here in the U.S.

- 1 cup canola or coconut oil
- 2 eggs
- 1 1/2 cups sugar
- 2 teaspoons vanilla
- 3/4 cup coconut flour
- 1 cup whole wheat or spelt flour
- 1 cup kamut® or triticale flour
- 1 teaspoon baking soda
- 1 teaspoon cinnamon
- 1/2 teaspoon salt
- 2 cups bananas, mashed
- 1 8-ounce can crushed pineapple, drained (reserve juice for icing)
- 1 cup shredded coconut

Icing/Glaze:
- Reserved pineapple juice
- 4 tablespoons cream cheese, softened
- 2 tablespoons powdered sugar
- Thin with milk or water for more of a glaze

Preheat oven to 350°. Using a hand or stand mixer, beat first four ingredients at high speed 2 minutes. Add bananas and pineapple, stir until combined. Sift dry ingredients into mixing bowl and mix until thoroughly combined. Gently fold in coconut. Do not overmix. Pour batter into two greased 8" round or square pans or one 9" by 13" pan. Bake 25-35 minutes until cake tests done. Let cake cool slightly before icing or glazing.

Never Death By Chocolate

... Especially if you are vegan. This vegan chocolate cake is moist and flavorful, reminiscent of the sour cream or mayonnaise cakes of the past. There is no guilt inside this cake as it contains a healthy dose of fiber and added nutrients of whole-grain flours. Double the recipe if two layers of cake are desired.

- 1/2 cup whole wheat or spelt flour
- 1/2 cup teff flour
- 1/2 cup buckwheat flour
- 1/3 cup cocoa powder
- 1 cup sugar
- 1 teaspoon soda
- 1/2 teaspoon salt
- 1 cup cold water
- 1/2 cup canola oil
- 1 tablespoon vinegar
- 1 teaspoon vanilla

Preheat oven to 350°. In a medium bowl combine all dry ingredients and whisk until thoroughly combined. Make a well in the center of the dry ingredients and add all remaining ingredients. Mix until smooth. Pour into greased 9" round or square cake pan. Bake 25-30 minutes or until cake tests done. I like it topped with whipped cream and chocolate shavings.

No Rules Chocolate Torte

- 2 1/2 cups cocoa powder
- 1 cup butter, softened
- 1 1/2 cups sugar
- 5 eggs
- 1 cup almond or hazelnut meal/flour
- 1 tablespoon vanilla

Preheat oven to 300°. Using a hand or stand mixer, beat all ingredients 3-5 minutes. Spoon into greased 8" cake or tart pan. Bake 25-30 minutes or until slightly firm. Do not overbake. Cool and top with ganache if desired.

Favorite Chocolate Ganache:
- 4 ounces dark, semisweet, milk, or white chocolate, chopped
- 1/2 cup half and half

In a small sauce pan on low to medium heat, melt chocolate in half and half. Whisk until smooth. Pour on cake and refrigerate immediately to set.

Following the rules works, but why go to the trouble of melting chocolate, softening butter at room temperature, separating eggs and folding in this and that, when you can throw it all into a bowl, mix it up and have a decadent dessert in 30 minutes? Either way you prepare it, this is chocolate bliss!

Luscious Lemon Poppy Seed

Resembling my very own wedding cake, this one adapts well to whole-grain flour.

Although great without the glaze, adding the tart glaze with zest is what makes this cake truly luscious.

- 1 cup sugar
- 1/2 cup butter
- 2 eggs
- 2 teaspoons lemon extract
- 1/2 cup sour cream or plain yogurt
- 1 1/2 cups whole wheat or spelt flour
- 1 teaspoon baking powder
- 1/2 teaspoon salt
- 2 tablespoons poppy seeds

Preheat oven to 350°. Using a hand or stand mixer, beat butter and sugar at high speed 1 minute. Add eggs and lemon extract, beating an additional minute. Mix in sour cream or yogurt. Sift flour, baking powder, and salt into mixing bowl and mix until thoroughly combined. Fold in poppy seeds. Pour batter into greased 9" round or square cake pan or two small loaf pans. Bake 30-35 minutes or until cake tests done. Drizzle with glaze while warm.

Sour Lemon Glaze:
- Juice and zest of 1 lemon
- 2 tablespoons powdered sugar

In a small bowl mix until sugar is dissolved.

Second Place Strawberry Tall Cake

*G*rowing up on a strawberry farm, it was tradition to set aside the first berries of the season to go into a scrumptious cake. When I was in 7th grade, my first cake was entered into a contest. Even though a friend of mine won first place with her fancy frosted rocking horse cake, my strawberry shortcake was the first one eaten! Both versions are great, but version #2 was developed for family members with wheat and dairy intolerances.

Shortcake #1:
- 1/2 cup sugar
- 1/2 cup butter
- 1 egg
- 3 teaspoons vanilla
- 3/4 cup milk
- 1 cup kamut® flour
- 1/2 cup whole wheat flour
- 1/2 cup brown rice flour
- 2 teaspoons baking powder
- 1/2 teaspoon salt

Shortcake #2:
- 1/2 cup olive oil
- 1/2 cup sugar
- 1 egg
- 1 teaspoon almond extract
- 3/4 cup soy milk
- 1 cup spelt flour
- 1/2 cup amaranth flour
- 1/2 cup quinoa flour
- 1 tablespoon cornstarch
- 2 teaspoons baking powder
- 1/2 teaspoon salt

For both cakes, preheat oven to 350°. In a medium bowl cream butter or oil and sugar. Add eggs and mix until smooth. Add milk and flavorings, mixing well. Sift dry ingredients into mixing bowl and mix until thoroughly combined. Do not overmix. Pour batter into two greased 9" round baking pans. Bake 25-30 minutes or until cake tests done. Cool completely. Layers can be split horizontally for more layers. Spoon strawberries and whip cream between each layer. Serve immediately.

Chocolate+Coffee=Cookie

Chewy and deep chocolate in flavor, these are an especially rich tasting cookie. They store, travel, and freeze well. I like to keep the dough in the freezer, wrapped in waxed paper formed into a log shape, ready to slice and cook at a moment's notice and serve to unexpected guests.

- 3/4 cup butter or coconut oil
- 2 cups brown sugar
- 3 eggs
- 2 teaspoons vanilla
- 3 tablespoons instant coffee or espresso
- 1 cup whole wheat flour or spelt
- 3/4 cup cocoa powder
- 1/2 cup quinoa flour
- 2 teaspoons baking powder
- 1/2 teaspoon salt
- 1 cup chocolate chunks or chips

Preheat oven to 350°. In a large bowl, cream together first four ingredients. Dissolve coffee in 1 tablespoon hot water and add to bowl. Mix dry ingredients in a separate bowl. Add dry ingredients to wet ingredients and stir until thoroughly combined. Add chips or chunks. Do not over stir. Drop by rounded teaspoonfuls on a baking sheet. Bake 8 minutes for a chewy cookie, 10 minutes for a crispy cookie.

Chai Latte Cookies

- 1 cup butter or coconut oil
- 1 cup sugar
- 2 eggs
- 2 teaspoons vanilla
- 1 1/2 cups brown rice flour
- 1 cup amaranth flour
- 4 tablespoons corn starch
- 4 tablespoons instant tea powder
- 3 teaspoons Chinese 5-spice
- 1 teaspoon soda
- 1 teaspoon salt
- 2 cups walnuts or pecans, finely chopped
- 1 cup white chocolate chips, chopped

Preheat oven to 350°. In a large bowl, cream together first four ingredients. Mix dry ingredients in a separate bowl. Add dry ingredients to wet ingredients and stir until smooth. Add chips and nuts. Do not over stir. Drop by rounded teaspoonfuls on a baking sheet. Bake 8 minutes for a chewy cookie, 10 minutes for a crispy cookie.

Traveling India instilled in me a love of anything "chai". The fresh, exotic spices always bring back wonderful memories of exciting travel adventures. Adding ginger or fresh-ground cardamom to these cookies makes a great flavor variation. Also almond or hazelnut meal/flour can be substituted for the finely chopped nuts. Being gluten free is an added bonus.

San Ginger Cookies

efinitely ginger to the third power. My first taste of crystalized ginger came while shopping in Beijing. Right after stuffing ourselves with a street-food meal of hot baked sweet potatoes, blood oranges and kebabs, we stumbled upon a bakery that had the most delicious ginger cookies. My version has a milder ginger flavor but feel free to amp' it up by adding extra ginger, in any form.

- 1 cup sugar
- 1/2 cup butter
- 2 tablespoons molasses
- 1 egg
- 1 tablespoon fresh ginger root, grated
- 1 cup spelt or whole wheat flour
- 1 cup triticale or kamut® flour
- 1/2 cup teff or buckwheat flour
- 1 1/2 teaspoons soda
- 1/2 teaspoon salt
- 2 teaspoons ginger
- 1/4 cup crystalized ginger, minced

Preheat oven to 350°. In a large bowl, cream together first five ingredients. Mix dry ingredients in a separate bowl. Add dry ingredients to wet ingredients and stir until smooth. Add crystalized ginger. Do not over stir. Drop by rounded teaspoonfuls on a baking sheet. Bake 8 minutes for a chewy cookie, 10 minutes for a crispy cookie.

Every Country's Cookie

- 1 cup butter, softened
- 1/2 cup powdered sugar
- 1 teaspoon vanilla or almond extract
- 1 1/4 cups whole wheat flour
- 1 cup oat or barley flour
- 1 cup almond or hazelnut meal/flour
- 1/2 teaspoon salt
- Powdered sugar for rolling

Preheat oven to 325°. In a large bowl, cream together first three ingredients. Mix dry ingredients in a separate bowl. Add dry ingredients to wet ingredients and stir until smooth. Do not over stir. Chill dough until firm. Roll into small balls and place on a baking sheet. Bake 10-12 minutes. Roll cookies in powdered sugar or sprinkle while warm. Place on racks to cool.

Many cultures claim these cookies. They are sometimes called Mexican Wedding Cookies, Russian Tea Cakes, or Snowballs. Like a puff of sweet flavor exploding in your mouth, I just call them good. Try different flavorings to produce different variations of this cookie.

Wheat-Free Vegan Cookies

When dining at a raw food restaurant in San Diego, my oldest son asked, "Where do vegans come from?" In all our discussions that evening about where to eat, we had bounced around from Japanese to Korean to Italian food, to vegetarian, vegan, and raw-food restaurants. What great dinner conversation that spurred...and no matter where you come from, you'll love these cookies.

- 1/2 cup maple syrup
- 1/3 cup canola oil
- 1/3 cup sugar
- 1 tablespoon molasses
- 1 teaspoon vanilla
- 1 cup spelt flour
- 1 cup quinoa flour
- 1/2 teaspoon soda
- 1/2 teaspoon baking powder
- 1/4 teaspoon salt
- 3/4 cup dark chocolate chips

Preheat oven to 350°. In a large bowl, cream together first five ingredients. Mix dry ingredients in a separate bowl. Add dry ingredients to wet ingredients and stir until smooth. Add chocolate chips. Do not over stir. Drop by rounded teaspoonfuls on a baking sheet. Bake 7 minutes for a chewy cookie, 8-9 minutes for a crispy cookie. Do not overbake.

Peanut Chewies

These gluten-free cookies can be made using any kind of nut, seed, or soy butter. Try other combinations of gluten-free flours such as millet, sorghum, corn, or quinoa. This recipe begs for experimentation.

- 2 cups peanut or other nut butter
- 1 1/2 cups sugar
- 2 eggs
- 1/2 cup brown rice flour
- 1/4 cup coconut flour

Preheat oven to 350°. In a large bowl, cream together peanut butter, eggs and sugar. Add flours to wet ingredients and stir well. Roll into small balls and place on baking sheet. Using a fork, press balls flat by making cross hash marks. Bake 8-9 minutes or until lightly browned. Do not overbake.

Dangerous Brownies

- 8 ounces unsweetened baking chocolate
- 1 cup butter
- 4 eggs
- 3 cups sugar
- 3 tablespoons vanilla
- 1/2 cup teff or buckwheat flour
- 1/2 cup barley or millet flour
- 1/2 cup whole wheat or spelt flour
- 1 teaspoon salt
- 2 cups chocolate chips of choice
- 2 cups nuts of choice (pecans and/or walnuts preferred)

Preheat oven to 350°. In a small sauce pan, melt chocolate with butter over low heat. Using a hand or stand mixer, beat eggs, sugar and vanilla at high speed 5-7 minutes. Sift dry ingredients into mixing bowl and mix until thoroughly combined. Add chocolate chips and/or nuts. Pour batter into a greased 9" by 13" pan. Bake 30-40 minutes or until set. Do not overbake. If they end up too gooey, put them in the freezer for an amazingly chewy "iced-brownie."

This brownie could go by many names... World's Best Brownies, Ultimate Brownies, To-Die-For Brownies (my son's favorite), How-to-Keep-a-Man Brownies (my husband's favorite). I just call them "dangerous" due to the fact that after making hundreds of batches of brownies in my lifetime, these are the ones I could not stay out of. They are that good!

Nuts About Shortbread

Holiday baking is something I look forward to every year. At my house the "holidays" start as soon as the Halloween candy gets turned over to the Great Pumpkin. Shortbread is a favorite to give as it stores well, freezes great, and tastes amazing!

- 1/2 cup butter, room temperature
- 1/4 cup brown sugar
- 1 teaspoon pure vanilla extract
- 1/2 teaspoon almond extract
- 1/2 cup whole wheat or spelt flour
- 1/4 cup fine yellow cornmeal
- 1/4 cup brown rice flour
- 1/4 cup almond or hazelnut meal/flour
- 1/4 teaspoon salt

Preheat oven to 300°. In a large bowl, cream together first four ingredients. Mix dry ingredients in a separate bowl. Add dry ingredients to wet ingredients and stir until thoroughly combined. Do not over stir. Press dough into a tart pan, prick with a fork in several places. Make impressions with a knife where you want to cut the cookies. Bake 30-40 minutes or until lightly golden.

Sorority Bars

I have never met a 7-Layer Bar I didn't like. It all started when I first tried them at the Alpha Chi Omega house at Oregon State University. For the next 20 years I would make many versions of this bar, depending on the ingredients I had in the pantry. This recipe has some great nutritious ingredients that stand up well to being doused in sweetened condensed milk.

- 1/2 cup butter, softened
- 1 cup brown sugar
- 2 eggs
- 1 cup whole wheat or spelt flour
- 1/2 cup oat flour
- 1/2 cup coconut flour
- 1/2 cup oatmeal or barley flakes
- 1/4 teaspoon salt
- 2 cups mixed nuts (walnuts, pecans, almonds and/or pistachios) chopped
- 1 cup coconut
- 3/4 cup butterscotch chips
- 3/4 cup chocolate chips
- 1 can sweetened condensed milk
- Cayenne pepper, optional

Preheat oven to 375°. In a large bowl, cream together first three ingredients. Mix dry ingredients in a separate bowl. Add dry ingredients to wet ingredients and stir until thoroughly combined. Press dough into a greased 9" by 13" pan. Bake 7 minutes. Remove from oven and evenly distribute remaining ingredients. Drizzle condensed milk over the top. For an additional taste sensation, sprinkle a bit of cayenne pepper over part or all of the bars. Bake an additional 15-20 minutes or until lightly golden.

S'more Cookies Please

*N*o longer do you have to wait until summer to enjoy the flavor of good, old-fashioned s'mores! Truthfully, I think traditional s'mores only taste good because it is summer time and more than likely, we are eating them while on a happy vacation. These bar cookies are much better than the real thing, and healthier too.

- 1/2 cup butter, room temperature
- 3/4 cup brown sugar
- 2 large eggs
- 1 tsp vanilla extract
- 3/4 cup whole wheat or spelt flour
- 1 cup graham flour
- 1/2 cup oat bran
- 1/2 cup flax meal
- 1/2 teaspoon baking soda
- 1/2 teaspoon salt
- 1 3.5-ounce chocolate bar, chopped
- 1 7-ounce jar marshmallow cream or 2 cups mini-marshmallows
- 1/4 cup graham crackers, crushed

Preheat oven to 350°. In a large bowl, cream together first four ingredients. Mix dry ingredients in a separate bowl. Add dry ingredients to wet ingredients and stir until thoroughly combined. Press dough into a greased 9" by 13" pan. Bake 10-12 minutes. Remove from oven and evenly distribute remaining ingredients over the top. Bake an additional 10-15 minutes or until marshmallow is lightly golden. Cool completely before cutting into bars.

Fanned Apple Tart

- 1/4 cup butter
- 1/4 cup sugar
- 1 egg
- 1/4 cup milk
- 2 teaspoons vanilla
- 1/2 cup whole wheat or spelt flour
- 1/2 cup quinoa flour
- 1/4 cup amaranth or garbanzo bean flour
- 1 1/2 teaspoons baking powder
- 1/2 teaspoon salt
- 5 cups apples, peeled and thinly sliced

Topping:
- 1/4 cup butter
- 1/4 cup sugar
- 1 teaspoon cinnamon

*T*his dessert can be made in any size pan and served in squares, rectangles, or pie wedges. Lovely topped with a dollop of freshly whipped cream or ice cream. Try with peaches, pears, or plums for a seasonal variation.

Preheat oven to 400°. In a large bowl, cream together first five ingredients. Mix dry ingredients in a separate bowl. Add dry ingredients to wet ingredients and stir until thoroughly combined. Press dough into a greased 9" by 13" pan or two round tart pans. Arrange apples in rows, covering the top of the tart. Sprinkle with cinnamon/sugar topping. Bake 35-45 minutes or until apples are tender. Cool slightly before cutting.

Pie or Cobbler?

When working with nutritious flours, some ideas start out as one thing and morph into another. Regardless, when they taste this good, no one seems to care. Much more flavorful than a traditional pie crust, this one can be adapted to almost any fruit. For the record, my clever husband wanted to name this one Pobbler! The crust can be used on the bottom or top of the pie.

Crust:

- 1 cup spelt or whole wheat flour
- 1/2 cup oat flour
- 1/2 cup barley or millet flour
- 1/3 cup canola or coconut oil
- 1/2 teaspoon salt
- 3 tablespoons cold water

In a small bowl mix flours and salt until well combined. Add oil and mix with a fork or pastry cutter until mixture resembles a fine crumb. Add water and work dough into a ball. On a lightly floured surface, or between sheets of waxed paper, roll with a floured rolling pin to 10"-12" in diameter.

Apple or Peach Filling:

- 6-8 cups apples or peaches, peeled and thinly sliced
- 1/2 cup sugar
- 1/4 cup spelt or whole wheat flour
- 1/2 teaspoon cinnamon
- Dash of salt
- 2 teaspoons lemon juice
- 3 tablespoons butter

Preheat oven to 400°. In a large bowl mix sugar, flour, cinnamon, and a dash of salt. Add fruit to flour mixture and toss gently. Sprinkle in lemon juice. Spoon fruit into pie pan. Divide butter into 6-8 thin slices and distribute evenly over fruit mixture. Place crust on top of fruit and secure to the edges of the pie pan. Make several slits in the top with a sharp knife to allow steam to escape. Bake 40-50 minutes. Place foil or a pie crust protector on the outside rim of the pan to prevent crust from overcooking.

Berrylicious Filling:

- 6-8 cups berries (Use one or a combination of several; blueberries, blackberries, raspberries, boysenberries, or sliced strawberries)
- 3/4 cup sugar
- 1/2 cup spelt or whole wheat flour
- Dash of salt
- 1 tablespoon lemon juice
- 3 tablespoons butter

Preheat oven to 400°. In a large bowl mix sugar, flour, and a dash of salt. Add fruit to flour mixture and toss gently. Sprinkle in lemon juice. Spoon fruit into pie pan. Divide butter into 6-8 thin slices and distribute evenly over fruit mixture. Place crust on top of fruit and secure to the edges of the pie pan. Make several slits in the top with a sharp knife to allow steam to escape. Bake 35-45 minutes. Place foil or a pie crust protector on the outside rim of the pan to prevent crust from overcooking.

Favorite Pumpkin

*A*t our house pumpkin pie can be found at any meal. Chock-full of vitamins, minerals, fiber, and antioxidants this super food is more than a sweet treat. We make it so much that my boys were making it by themselves at five years old.

Crust:
- 1 1/2 cup spelt or whole wheat flour
- 1 cup brown rice flour
- 1/2 cup canola or olive oil
- 1 teaspoon salt
- 2 tablespoons cold water

In a small bowl mix flours and salt until well combined. Add oil and mix with a fork or pastry cutter until mixture resembles a fine crumb. Add water and work dough into a ball. On a lightly floured surface, roll with a floured rolling pin to 10"-12" in diameter. Place crust in pie pan and secure edges.

Pumpkin Filling:
- 3 eggs
- 1/2 cup sugar
- 1 1/2 teaspoons cinnamon
- 1/2 teaspoon salt
- 1/2 teaspoon ginger
- 1/4 teaspoon cloves
- 1 16-ounce can pumpkin puree (or sweet potato or winter squash puree)
- 1 12-ounce can evaporated milk

Preheat oven to 425°. In a large bowl cream eggs, sugar, and spices. Whisk in pumpkin and milk. Place uncooked pie shell in pie pan and secure to the edges. Pour pumpkin filling into shell. Bake 15 minutes at 425°, lower heat to 350° and cook an additional 45 minutes or until pie is set. Chill before serving with whipped cream.

Razzle Me Dazzle Me Crunch

Topping:
- 1 cup oatmeal
- 1/2 cup sugar
- 1/3 cup flax meal
- 1/3 cup brown rice or coconut flour
- 1 teaspoon cinnamon or 1/2 teaspoon nutmeg
- 1/4 teaspoon salt
- 1/2 cup butter, melted

In a medium bowl mix dry ingredients. Add butter and mix with a fork until mixture resembles medium size crumbles.

Razzle Dazzle Filling:
- 1/3 cup sugar
- 1/3 cup brown rice flour
- 1/2 teaspoon nutmeg (optional)
- Dash of salt
- 3 cups raspberries
- 3 cups mango, peeled and cubed
- 2 tablespoons lemon juice

Preheat oven to 375°. In a large bowl mix sugar, flour, nutmeg, and a dash of salt. Add fruit to flour mixture and toss gently. Sprinkle in lemon juice. Spoon fruit into 8" by 8" pan. Evenly distribute crunch mixture over the top of the fruit. Bake 35-40 minutes or until crust is lightly golden.

Watch out with this topping as undisciplined children (or mothers-in-law) might sneak it off the dessert before it can be served...yes, Braxton, Kazden, and Jean, I am talking to you! Try it with the apple or peach pie filling or any of the berry pie fillings.

Blue Corn Bluebarb Crumble

Bluebarb is one word that will get my boys out of the swimming pool in a split second. Blessed with a very prolific rhubarb plant and lots of blueberry bushes, it's a summer-time favorite. The crumble topping is great with any of the other fruit fillings in this section.

Topping:
- 1/2 cup oat bran, flax meal, or wheat germ
- 1/2 cup biscuit mix or pancake mix
- 1/2 cup sugar
- 1/4 cup blue corn flour
- 1/4 cup butter, softened or 2 tablespoons olive or coconut oil
- 1/4 cup coconut oil
- 1 teaspoon vanilla

In a medium bowl mix dry ingredients. Add butter, oil, and vanilla and mix with a fork until mixture resembles large crumbles.

Bluebarb Filling:
- 1 1/2 cups sugar
- 2/3 cup whole wheat or spelt flour
- 1/2 teaspoon cinnamon or nutmeg
- Dash of salt
- 3 cups blueberries or blackberries
- 3 cups rhubarb, finely chopped

Preheat oven to 375°. In a large bowl mix sugar, flour, spices, and a dash of salt. Add fruit to flour mixture and toss gently. Spoon fruit into 9" by 13" pan. Evenly distribute crumble mixture over the top of the fruit. Bake 35-40 minutes or until crumble is lightly golden.

Orchard Crisp

Topping:
- 3/4 cup powdered sugar
- 1/3 cup amaranth or coconut flour
- 2 cups brown rice flour
- 2 teaspoons baking powder
- 1 teaspoon salt
- 2 teaspoons vanilla or 1 teaspoon almond extract
- 1/2 cup butter, melted

In a medium bowl mix dry ingredients. Add butter and vanilla or almond extract, and mix with a fork until mixture resembles fine crumbles.

Orchard Fruit Filling:
- 8-10 cups apples, peaches, plums, or pears (or a combination thereof), peeled and thinly sliced
- 1/2 cup sugar
- 1/3 cup quinoa or coconut flour
- 1 teaspoon Chinese 5-spice or pumpkin pie spice
- Dash of salt
- 1 tablespoon lemon juice
- 3 tablespoons butter

Preheat oven to 375°. In a large bowl mix sugar, flour, spices, and a dash of salt. Add fruit to flour mixture and toss gently. Spoon fruit into 9" by 13" pan. Evenly distribute crisp mixture over the top of the fruit. Bake 30-45 minutes or until crisp is lightly browned and fruit is tender. If the crisp gets brown before the fruit is done, cover with foil and continue cooking.

Grandpa is famous in the neighborhood for his apple crisp recipe. This recipe stirred things up a bit at the last family barbecue... move over grandpa, there's a new recipe in town and it's gluten free! To taste more like grandpa's, use only apples.

APPENDIX A

Nutritious Flours

The following list of flours are becoming more available every day. Each can be ordered on the Internet and many can be found in the baking section of some supermarkets and most health food stores.

Amaranth: (gluten free) high in protein, fiber, calcium, iron, zinc and vitamin E – grassy smell, tastes almost spicy.

Barley: (low gluten) high in soluble fiber, niacin, iron – adds a chewy texture, slightly nutty flavor.

Bean Flours: (gluten free) high in fiber, protein, folic acid – adds a nice consistency and a nutritional boost to cookies and quick breads.

Brown Rice Flour: (gluten free) high fiber, manganese, selenium, and B-vitamins – mildly flavored, works well in part of any recipe.

Buckwheat: (gluten free) high in protein, calcium, magnesium, phosphorous, B-vitamins, and iron – adds a malty, nutty flavor, a wholesome taste.

Coconut Flour: (gluten free) highest fiber content and lowest carbohydrate count of any flour, high protein, relatively hypoallergenic – slightly sweet but no deep coconut flavor, complements any recipe.

Corn Meal/Flour: (gluten free) high in fiber, vitamin A, manganese, potassium, and foliate; blue cornmeal is higher in protein than yellow – adds a great crunch to any recipe.

Graham Flour: coarsely ground wheat flour, high fiber, protein, iron B-vitamins, mineral rich – adds a slight crunch and pleasant sandiness to any recipe.

Green Pea Flour: (gluten free) high in fiber, protein, folic acid – adds a nice consistency and a nutritional boost to cookies and quick breads.

Kamut® Flour: (high gluten) very high in protein, potassium, B-vitamins, vitamin E, zinc, magnesium, and iron – tastes similar to white flour, can be used as a full-flour substitute.

Millet Flour: (gluten free) high in iron, potassium, protein, magnesium, calcium, phosphorous, manganese, zinc, B-vitamins, and fiber – easy to digest with a low allergen level.

Nut Meals/Flours: (gluten free) finely ground nuts; high in protein, fiber – can be finely ground at home using raw almonds, hazelnuts, cashews, pecans, walnuts, macadamia nuts.

Oat Flour: (sometimes gluten-free) high in fiber, B-vitamins, vitamin E, and many minerals – easy to digest.

Quinoa Flour: (gluten free) highest protein content of all flours and very high in many minerals, B-vitamins, and vitamin E; it is the only flour to contain all 9 essential amino acids which makes it a complete protein – can be used as a full-flour substitute.

Rye Flour: high in fiber, protein, iron, B-vitamins, vitamin E, and many other minerals – nutty flavor producing darker breads.

Sorghum Flour: (gluten free) high in protein and minerals – adds a slightly sweet flavor to baked goods.

Soy Flour: (gluten free) high in protein, fiber, iron, potassium, calcium, and foliate fiber – soy offers many additional health benefits.

Spelt Flour: (high gluten) high protein, B-vitamins, minerals, and fiber – tastes almost exactly like whole wheat, can be used as a full-flour substitute.

Teff Flour: (gluten free) high in fiber, calcium, iron, potassium, magnesium, zinc, and thiamin – adds a wholesome flavor much like buckwheat, produces a very dark bread.

Triticale Flour: (low gluten) combination of wheat and rye; high protein, fiber, thiamin, and minerals – mild in flavor, can be used as a full-flour substitute.

Whole Wheat: (high gluten) high fiber, protein, iron, B-vitamins, and minerals – replace any white flour recipe with whole wheat flour adding slightly less flour to accommodate the higher fiber content.

APPENDIX B

Recipe Rescue

If a quick bread, cake, or yeast bread doesn't turn out for me, I have a great trick. It becomes fried bread. My family loves this as a warm breakfast treat (if low in sugar) or as a dessert. This technique remedies bread that is too dry and crumbly or too moist and soggy. It also does wonders for stale cinnamon rolls or donuts (just slice them horizontally).

Simply slice bread or cake in 1/2" slices. Butter or oil a hot skillet or griddle. On medium heat toast the bread or cake on both sides, about 1 minute per side or until lightly browned. Serve immediately.

Another recipe rescue for yeast breads is croutons. There are two ways to make croutons. The first way is to cut bread in cubes and toast in a well-greased skillet. Season while toasting. Another way is to place bread cubes in a large sealable plastic bag and drizzle olive oil and spices into the bag. Toss to coat and place on a baking sheet. Toast bread in the oven at 400° until crunchy.

Tips for Bread Machine Bread

• The first thing I like to do with a new bread machine is follow the included recipe for basic white bread (I know, I know, I am promoting nutritious flours here; it's just a one-time deal!). This helps me to see how the machine works and if it is working properly.

• If bread dough looks too dry or crumbly or is not coming together to form a ball, add additional liquid, one tablespoon at a time.

• If bread dough looks more like batter in the first 5-10 minutes of mixing, add additional flour, one tablespoon at a time.

• If bread sinks in the middle or has large air pockets, cut down on the liquid next time.

• If bread is too dry and crust is tough, not enough liquid was used. When experimenting remember that if other whole grains, or dried fruit, is added, it will use up the liquid the bread needs.

• If bread doesn't rise, check for expired yeast.

• Don't be afraid to experiment. The term "artisan bread" will get you through any outcome. And don't expect breads baked with whole, nutritious flours to come out like fluffy, but tasteless, light white bread. Nutritious flours give you flavorful nutrients you WANT to taste.

• Remember that bread machines are not just for baking a finished loaf of bread. I actually use mine more often on the dough cycle for rolls, pizza crust, bread sticks and European style breads.

APPENDIX C

Fats & Fat Substitutes
- 1 cup equivalent of butter, margarine, whipped spreads (approved for baking), or shortening equals:
- 7/8 cup oil (vegetable, canola, corn, olive, peanut, coconut)
- 3/4 cup mayonnaise, sour cream or yogurt + 1/4 cup oil
- 1/2 cup applesauce + 1/2 cup oil
- 1/2 cup avocado or date puree + 1/3 cup oil

Sweeteners
- 1 cup white sugar, brown sugar equals:
- 1 1/3 cup powdered sugar
- 3/4 cup honey, date syrup, corn syrup or pure maple syrup
- 1 cup sucanat, palm sugar, maple sugar

Liquids
- 1 cup milk, buttermilk, soy milk, almond milk, rice milk equals:
- 2/3 cup evaporated milk + 1/3 cup water
- 3/4 cup plain yogurt + 1/4 cup water
- 3/4 cup pureed cottage cheese + 1/4 cup milk or water
- 3/4 cup sour cream + 1/4 cup milk or water

When making substitutions out of choice or desperation, I always make a note of what I did on the recipe card or page. Some of my favorite recipes have morphed over the years to include healthier ingredients and it's all due to experimentation. Keep in mind however, some substitutions may not produce the desired effects. Make a note of these as well, so you don't try it again.

APPENDIX D (see Index for page number)

Gluten-Free Recipes
- Peas In A Pod Soup
- Get Nutty Soup
- Longevity Soup
- Jet-Lag Soup
- All Salads (for Hideaway Bread Salad use gluten-free bread)
- Gluten-Free Taste-Full
- Gluten-Free Tortillas
- Sand Dollars
- Chick Dippers
- No Rules Chocolate Torte
- Chai Latte Cookies
- Peanut Chewies

Wheat-Free Recipes
- Peas In A Pod Soup
- Get Nutty Soup
- Tortilla Soup
- Longevity Soup
- Jet-Lag Soup
- Soup Sticks (use spelt flour)
- All Salads (for Hideaway Bread Salad use a wheat-free bread)
- Green Pea Pasta (use spelt flour)
- Lycopene Pizza-Pasta (use spelt flour)
- Confetti Bread (use spelt flour)
- Autumn Harvest Muffins (use spelt flour)
- Ginger Powered Muffins (use spelt flour and flax meal)
- Cheesy Drops (use spelt flour)
- Happy Hybrid Bread
- Whole, Dark & Handsome (use spelt flour)
- Not-For-The-Birds (use spelt flour)
- Gluten-Free Taste-Full
- Flat's Where It's At (use spelt flour)
- Funky Monkey (use spelt flour)
- Newlywed Rolls (use spelt flour)
- Mas Tortillas Por Favor
- Pancake Day Banana Pancakes (use spelt flour)
- Wheat-Free All-Week Pancake Mix
- African Pancakes
- 'LOVE'ly Waffles (use spelt flour)
- Time For Tea Biscuits (use spelt flour)

- Black & Blue Biscotti (use spelt flour)
- Sand Dollars
- Sweet Thins (use wheat-free suggestions)
- Cookies For Snack Again! (use wheat-free suggestions)
- Chocolate "Guess" cookies (use spelt flour)
- You Can Never Be Too Thin Or Too Crispy (use spelt flour)
- Power Balls (use wheat-free suggestions)
- Sweetie Pie Honey Bunches (use wheat-free suggestions)
- High-Protein Bars (use wheat-free suggestions)
- Go-Go Bars (use wheat-free suggestions)
- Dark Bread Crackers (use spelt flour)
- Snacker Crackers (use spelt flour)
- Chick Dippers
- Crispy Critters (use spelt flour)

- Secret P Cake (use spelt flour)
- Bukkitinggi Cake (use spelt flour)
- Never Death By Chocolate (use spelt flour)
- Luscious Lemon Poppy Seed (use spelt flour)
- No Rules Chocolate Torte
- Second Place Strawberry Tall Cake (Short Cake #2)
- Chocolate+Coffee=Cookie (use spelt flour)
- Chai Latte Cookies
- San Ginger Cookies
- Wheat-Free Vegan Cookies
- Peanut Chewies
- Nuts About Shortbread (use spelt flour)
- Dangerous Brownies (use spelt flour)
- Sorority Bars (use spelt flour)
- Fanned Apple Tart (use spelt flour)
- Pie or Cobbler? (use spelt flour)
- Razzle Me, Dazzle Me Crunch
- Orchard Crisp

Vegan Recipes

- Get Nutty Soup
- Longevity Soup
- Jet-Lag Soup
- All Salads (for Hideaway Bread Salad use a buttermilk substitute or soy milk)
- Gluten-Free Taste-Full
- Eat Your Veggies Bread
- Whole, Dark & Handsome
- Not-For-The-birds (use milk substitute)
- Hideaway Bread (use a buttermilk substitute or soy milk)
- Olive You Bread
- Tomorrow Bread

- Flat's Where It's At
- Outside-In Pizza
- Mas Tortillas Por Favor
- African Pancakes
- Power Balls (substitute appropriately)
- Dark Bread Crackers
- Snacker Crackers
- Chick Dippers
- Crispy Critters (use vegan-butter substitute)
- Never Death By Chocolate
- Wheat-Free Vegan Cookies
- Orchard Crisp

INDEX

OTHER COOKBOOKS BY TIFFANY AND SCOTT HAUGEN

Plank Cooking: The Essence of Natural Wood
by Scott & Tiffany Haugen

In Plank Cooking: The Essence of Natural Wood, globe-trotting authors, Scott & Tiffany Haugen, share some of the world's most exquisite flavors. Thai red curry prawns, Achiote pork roast, pesto couscous stuffed chicken, and caramelized bananas are just a few of the unique recipes brought to life in this fully illustrated, one-of-a-kind book. This book outlines how to master the art of plank cooking, from seasoning planks to detailed cooking tips in over 100 easy-to-follow recipes. Though exotic tastes prevail, the ingredients used in Plank Cooking are easy to find in most grocery stores. 6 x 9 inches, 152 pages, all-color.

      Spiral SB: **$19.95**   ISBN-13: 978-1-57188-332-2   UPC: 0-81127-00164-4

Grill It! Plank It! Wrap It! Smoke It!
by Tiffany Haugen

Packed with flavorful, healthy, family-friendly recipes and creative techniques, this all-in-one book shares all that you need to know about grilling, plank and wrap cooking, and smoking foods. Each cooking style includes appetizers, vegetables, meats, seafood, and desserts. Marinades, rubs, salsas, and sauces are also featured. This is the first book to combine these three styles of cooking into one convenient and attractive book. 6 x 9 inches, 156 pages, all-color.

      Spiral SB: **$19.95**   ISBN-13: 978-1-57188-416-9   UPC: 0-81127-00250-4

Smoking Salmon & Steelhead
by Scott & Tiffany Haugen

Among the many benefits of fishing is the chance to bring home the occasional salmon for the smoker. But are you tired of using the same old recipe? If so, the Haugens have done all the experimenting for you. The result is this book, filled with 54 wet and dry brine recipes, including: sweet teriyaki, tropical tang, extra hot habenero, sweet & simple, chardonnay splash, spicy sweet, triple pepper, and many, many more. They also share great tips on different smoking woods to use, preparation prior to smoking your fish, cannon smoked salmon, their favorite recipes using smoked salmon, and a section on troubleshooting meant to answer basic questions. 6 x 9 inches, 96 pages, all-color.

      Spiral SB: **$19.95**   ISBN-13: 978-1-57188-290-5   UPC: 0-81127-00119-4

Cooking Salmon & Steelhead: Exotic Recipes From Around the World
by Scott & Tiffany Haugen

This is not your grandmother's salmon cookbook. The long-time favorites are in-cluded and also unique yet easy-to-prepare dishes, like Cabo fish tacos and Tuscan pesto. This cookbook includes: Appetizers, soups & salads, entrees, one-dish meals, exotic tastes, marinades & rubs, outdoor cooking, pastas, stuffed fish, plank cook-ing, wine selection, scaling and fileting your catch, choosing market fish, cooking tips, and so much more. The Haugens have traveled to and studied cuisines in countries around the world—including the Caribbean, Asia, and Europe—your kitchen is not complete without a copy of Cooking Salmon & Steelhead. 6 x 9 inches, 184 pages, all-color.

      Spiral SB: **$24.95**   ISBN-13: 978-1-57188-291-2   UPC: 0-81127-00120-0

Ask for these titles at your local bookstore, if unavailable call toll-free to order 1-800-541-9498 or go to our website amatobooks.com.